COPING WITH VIOLENCE
A Guide for the Human Services

VAUGHAN BOWIE

KARIBUNI PRESS

SYDNEY

1989

Coping with Violence: A Guide for the Human Services
Karibuni Press
P.O. Box 555
Campbelltown N.S.W. Australia.

Vaughan Bowie B.S.S., M.Sc., M.A.
Lecturer, School of Community and Welfare Studies,
University of Western Sydney Macarthur

First published March 1989 by Karibuni Press,
Second printing May 1989
Third printing August 1990

Printed in Australia by Rotary Offset Press, Homebush.

National Library of Australia, Cataloguing-in-Publication Data

Bowie, Vaughan, 1950–   .
        Coping with violence.

        Bibliography.
        Includes index.
        ISBN 1 875170 01 4.

        1.   Human services personnel – Crimes against.
        2.   Violence – Prevention.
        3.   Human services personnel – Training of.
        I.   Title.

361.3'2

CONTENTS

Chapter Four. Principles of Physical Intervention.....51

Chapter Five. The 'SACRED' Approach To Managing Aggression 85

List of Figures and Pictures

Acknowledgments & Dedication

My thanks to Macarthur Institute and the School of Community and Welfare Studies for their generous financial and resource support and especially to Don Robertson for his budgeting skills and practical encouragement.

Further thanks to the New South Wales Premiers Department for also supporting financially this project through the International Year of Peace Secretariat.

I acknowledge my debt to the following authors Paul Smith, Stanley Bute, George Thompson, Terry Dobson and Michael Thackery whose ideas have been extensively used and modified in this book. The publishers, J.P. Tarcher Inc., graciously gave permission to reproduce the chapter *A Soft Answer*, from the book *Safe and Alive*, by Terry Dobson and Judith Shepherd-Chow, copyright 1981.

The illustrations and cover were designed by Lynne White, the photography by Nerrida and Kevin Rosolen, and modelling by Deirdre and Vaughan Bowie, Rob O'Neill and Graeme Rendell. Ken Rolph edited and typeset the text.

Finally to my wife, Deirdre, who has typed, proof read and 'computerised' large sections of the text, thank you.

I would also like to dedicate this book to fellow Human Service Workers and friends in South Africa, The Middle East, Northern Ireland and The Bronx, New York and to those workers who have paid the supreme cost while caring for others.

Foreword

This excellent and important volume will do much to contribute to a greatly neglected area—one which, as the author indicates, is often denied in its significance to human service workers and organisations, as indeed it has been in the past for most of those who have been victims of violence.

While it is clear that societies must confront, understand and do all they can to prevent violence and its consequences, it is also inevitable that many individuals, particularly those in human service organisations will often have to deal with situations where violence is a possibility or a fact. Bowie's review of the few studies documenting violence experienced by human service workers shows that such direct personal experience is certainly not infrequent. Distress, impaired functioning, post traumatic stress reaction and disorder, worker depression and burnout, are all possible consequences of such an experience.

It is critical for all organisations involving human service workers, be they private or government, institutional or community based, to address these issues. This book provides information on the understanding of violence and its possible origins, the interpersonal and other techniques, particularly verbal and negotiative, for defusing and preventing violent outcomes as well as the training and support systems needed. The importance for organisations rests in their ability to develop education and staff training opportunities. This will help prevent and mitigate situations of violence and enable workers to deal with them in the best possible way through the provision of access to staff debriefing, employee assistance and staff support programmes. Such systematic preventive approaches speak out also for the ethos of the organisation and reflect approaches which are likely to enhance staff morale, lessen the likelihood that violent episodes will develop and prevent staff loss and burnout, thus ultimately improving the human and economic efficiency and service of the system.

A constructive approach to issues of violence recognises and sympathetically integrates what is known about causes. Bowie identifies the anger at loss and injustice which is so frequently the vector of many, many social and personal factors including, as well, those variables of mental illness and physical and other impairments. The facts of this volume are encompassed in the true story of the opening and closing chapters— the comparison between the 'hard' and the 'soft' answers to violence, which will do much to help human service personnel in this sometimes frightening, difficult and challenging part of their work.

Workers reading this volume will find much that is of practical assistance, as well as a reassuring and reality based approach. The fears an individual faces in a violent situation are many— the threat of personal injury, the terror and fear of loss of their life and those they love, the loss of a sense of personal invulnerability as well as the hurt and anger. These are but some of the complex reactions that must be dealt with when one is threatened or assaulted by those who are the recipients of one's care and help.

There are special issues too, depending not only on the worker's own background and experience, but also social, cultural and gender variables. For women in situations of actual threat, fear, especially of rape and sexual assault and reflexes of submission, may override any intellectual understanding of the situation. For men issues of face, personal aggression and dominance may conflict with peaceful and negotiative intent. Each person needs to understand their own agenda, their pattern of experience, and if the trauma of violence occurs, the professional resources available to deal with it. At the time of any such crisis there is not only the need for support and the opportunity to talk through what has happened with those who may have experienced a similar occurrence, but also sensitive appreciation by fellow workers and family that will help the worker regain the needed sense of mastery and integrity. Through this the worker will be helped to deal with the experience in ways which lessen their pain, but at the same time enable them to draw strength from having survived and integrated what has happened.

It is not a good feeling to be threatened or hurt when we are trying to help others— it is frightening and painful for us and our families. Yet the understanding of this book can help us to face such crisis and come to terms with them. It is an honest and helpful approach, relevant for all human service workers.

Beverly Raphael
Professor of Psychiatry
University of Queensland.
Australia.

Introduction

This book aims to help Human Service Workers cope with and defuse aggression and violence they experience while performing their duties.

The definition of a Human Service Worker used here is purposely broad, including people in a range of public contact positions. These can include service delivery, such as housing and employment staff, care givers including doctors, nurses, welfare and social workers, recreational, community and youth workers. They can also include teachers, police and correctional officers and court officials. All have the common factor of face to face contact, of an often stressful type, with members of the public or those in some types of 'care' situations.

The book outlines the skills needed by those in institutional or residential care situations as well as those based in community settings or undertaking home visits. Additional information is given for those working in the latter, less structured helping situations.

The book aims to teach practical, common sense principles for the prevention and defusion of violence and post trauma support of assaulted workers. It is practical in its orientation but also supplies some helpful theoretical background information that the reader can pursue in more detail through the attached references.

Prevention, defusion and post trauma support skills are not frequently part of training for Human Service Workers and this book hopes to be a partial remedy to this lack of training. It does not just provide a list of does and don'ts but rather aims to teach workers the skills to analyse and intervene in situations using underlying principles applied with good judgment and common sense. However, no book can teach all the skills needed to prevent or defuse situations of violence or replace the need to use plain common sense.

The approaches outlined need to be constantly practised, modified and upgraded by the workers themselves and though these approaches have worked in practice, the author can make no guarantee that the techniques outlined will prevent or avoid any injury or loss to those using these methods. Workers use these techniques at their own risk and assume full responsibility for any injury or loss arising from the use of these methods in any setting whatsoever.

There has been only limited research done on the effectiveness of such training programs for workers in the areas of prevention, defusion and support. However, this research seems to indicate an increase in workers' ability and confidence in dealing with situation of violence after such training (Infantino and Musingo 1985).

An attempt is not made in this book to define aggression and violence in a tight, consistent fashion, but rather as a summary of the numerous ways they are defined by researchers, authors and the general public. Siann (1985) attempts such a summary by describing aggression as involving an intention to hurt or emerge superior to others but without necessarily involving physical injury. Such behaviour may or may not be regarded as having underlying motives. Siann defines violence as involving the use of great force or physical intensity often impelled by an aggressive motivation.

Such 'traditional' definitions of violence attempt to be objective in outlining the nature and motivation for the attack. However, there is also a need to be able to measure and understand the 'subjective' impact, both immediately and in the long term, of violence against workers when attempting to provide appropriate support services.

For purposes of definition in this book, verbal assaults, threats and intimidations will all be included as part of aggression, while physical assault and damage will be classified as violence. Note that the definition used here is not necessarily the same as those used by other authors and researchers.

Problems of definition are rife in the research material on the topic of violence against Human Service Workers. Great caution must therefore be exercised in attempting comparisons to, or drawing guidelines for practice from, the mentioned research.

Chapter One, in a novel way, outlines an initial attempt by Terry Dobson to resolve a situation of escalating violence in a rather inappropriate manner. The reader is left until the final chapter to see how this situation is surprisingly resolved.

Chapter Two explores the extent of violence in the workplace as well as some possible reasons for its presence and the particular forms in which it shows itself.

Chapter Three deals with the key verbal and non-verbal skills needed to communicate in crisis situations while Chapter Four outlines the principles of physical intervention and the approaches needed for community based contacts.

Chapter Five brings together in a particular framework, the S.A.C.R.E.D. approach, the particular strategies needed to prevent or defuse a situation of aggression or violence against workers.

Chapter Six outlines the personal and social costs to workers of being victims of aggression and violence, while Chapter Seven deals with one particular response by workers to violence, that of depression.

Chapter Eight gives guidelines for the provision of prevention and post trauma services and employee assistance programs.

Finally, Chapter Nine emphasises through the continuation of Chapter One that the best answer to violence is usually 'a soft answer'.

The author finishes the book with a personal conclusion, encouraging society as a whole to deal with the problem of violence.

Chapter One. A Soft Answer (part one)

A turning point in my life came one day on a train in the suburbs of Tokyo in the middle of a drowsy spring afternoon. The old car clanking and rattling over the rails was comparatively empty— a few housewives with their kids in tow, some old folks out shopping, a couple of off-duty bartenders studying the racing form. I gazed absently at the drab houses and dusty hedgerows.

At one station the doors opened and suddenly the quiet afternoon was shattered by a man bellowing at the top of his lungs, yelling violent, obscene, incomprehensible curses. Just as the door closed, the man, still yelling, staggered into our car. He was big, drunk, and dirty, dressed in labourers clothing. His bulging eyes were demonic, neon red. His hair was crusted with filth. Screaming, he swung at the first person he saw, a woman holding a baby. The blow glanced off her shoulder, sending her spinning into the laps of an elderly couple. It was a miracle that the baby was unharmed.

The terrified couple jumped up and scrambled toward the other end of the car. The labourer aimed a kick at the retreating back of the old lady, but he missed and she scuttled to safety. This so enraged the drunk that he grabbed the metal pole in the center of the car and tried to wrench it out of its stanchion. I could see that one of his hands was cut and bleeding. The train lurched ahead, the passengers frozen with fear.

I stood up. At the time, I was young, in pretty good shape, was six feet tall and weighed 225 pounds. I'd been putting in a solid eight hours of Aikido training every day for the past three years and thought I was tough. The trouble was, my martial skill was untested in actual combat. As a student of Aikido, I was not allowed to fight.

My teacher, the founder of Aikido, taught us each morning that the art was devoted to peace. "Aikido," he said again and again, "is the art of reconciliation. Whoever has the mind to fight has broken his connection with the universe. If you try to dominate other people, you are already defeated. We study how to resolve conflict, not how to start it."

I listened to his words. I tried hard. I wanted to quit fighting. I had even gone so far as to cross the street a few times to avoid the *chimpira*, the pinball punks who lounged around the train stations. They'd have been happy to test my martial ability. My forbearance exalted me. I felt tough and holy. In my heart of hearts, however, I was dying to be a hero. I wanted a chance, an absolutely legitimate opportunity whereby I might save the innocent by destroying the guilty.

"This is it!" I said to myself as I got to my feet. "This slob, this animal, is drunk and mean and violent. People are in danger. If I don't do something fast, someone will probably get hurt."

Seeing me stand up, the drunk saw a chance to focus his rage. "Aha!" he roared. "A foreigner! You need a lesson in Japanese manners!" He punched the metal pole once to give weight to his words.

Hanging on lightly to the commuter strap overhead, I gave him a slow look of disgust and dismissal— every bit of nastiness I could summon up. I planned to take this turkey apart, but he had to be the one to move first. And I wanted him mad, because the madder he got, the more certain my victory. I pursed my lips and blew him a sneering, insolent kiss that hit him like a slap in the face. "All right!" he hollered. "You're gonna get a lesson." He gathered himself for a rush at me. He would never know what hit him.

Chapter Two. The High Cost of Caring

Violence in the Workplace

Since the late 1970s, there has been increasing concern by trade unions, health and safety committees, researchers and Human Service Workers at the apparently increasing number of severe assaults against those in face to face helping situations. Despite the genuine concern about this perceived increase in violent assaults, there has been little research undertaken to test these claims. The first part of this chapter will summarise current research from the United Kingdom, the United States and Australia.

Research in the United Kingdom

In the United Kingdom, the Industrial Relations Services (1979), while stating that there was no clear evidence that attacks on employees were increasing, went on to rank what they perceived as the types of workers most at risk of assault. In their study the highest ranked were hospital employees, especially nurses in casualty departments or psychiatric hospitals. Next were ambulance personnel, then residential care workers, Department of Health and Social Security counter staff, Department of Employment staff and finally local Government employees such as rent collectors, gardeners, home helps and car park attendants.

In 1981, the National and Local Government Officers' Association (NALGOA), surveyed their members on the question of assault. The main categories of staff identified as at risk were housing and social service workers and inspection and enforcement staff. Injuries received ranged from verbal abuse to property damage, stabbing and death. The workers reported a wide, often unsatisfactory, variation in responses by employers to such incidents.

The numbers of staff prepared to report incidents of violence is also of some note. In a survey of all the social service departments in Great Britain for reported violence against workers (Rowett 1986), there was only one reported case of violence against a social worker from a sample of 259 social workers. However, a detailed follow-up study of all social workers in one local council area found that one in four had been the victim of violence, indicating possible gross under-reporting of incidents in the other government areas.

The UK research (Brown, Bute & Ford, 1979; Rowett, 1986; Weiner & Crosby, 1986) has also generally indicated that day care and residential workers face a greater number of violent incidents than do fieldworkers. This may be because residential and day care workers are in greater continuous contact with service users and often do not have an easy exit option, as do fieldworkers. Also fieldworkers are likely to be more highly trained than other types of workers.

However, it should be noted that the severity of episodes experienced by workers in the day care and residential settings may be somewhat less than that experienced by field workers. In the UK research, although fieldworkers reported lesser amounts of violence, most of the six fatalities in recent years have occurred amongst fieldworkers.

During the last ten years there has also been one fatality each for social workers in Sweden, France, Denmark and Israel (Swedish Union of Social Workers 1987).

Research in the United States

The other major source of information and research that is readily available on violence against people helpers comes from the United States. While the British research tends to focus on residential care workers and community based workers, the U.S. data appears to be more centred on mental health personnel, general health and welfare staff, therapists in private practice and police.

Recent research into assaults against psychiatrists and other therapists has reported rates of assault ranging from 20% to

74% with a mean of 42%. Such rates are probably only a percentage of the actual rates due to under-reporting of actual incidents. (Thackery, 1987a).

Kalogerakis (1971) was one of the first to gather information on violent incidents in the US. His research focused on the years 1964–1969 and noted that most reported incidents of aggression were of a minor nature and mainly involved nursing staff.

During the 1970s, research in the area began to shift more towards therapists (i.e. psychiatrists, social workers, psychologists, counsellors). A survey by Madden and others (1976) found that 48 of 115 surveyed psychiatrists had been assaulted a total of 68 times. 53% of those attacked felt that they had played some part in provoking the attack. These psychiatrists were most often attacked when working in high risk settings, such as emergency rooms and prisons, and in the early stages of their careers.

Whitman, Armao & Dent (1976) studied attacks on psychiatrists, psychologists and social workers. They found that during 1972, 1.9% of patients/clients threatened their therapists, and 0.63% actually attacked the therapist. Of the sample of 101 therapists, 24% were attacked during that year and 74% described at least one incident of assault against them.

Bernstein's research (1981), surveyed 422 therapists on the experience of assault. 14.2% of those surveyed indicated that they had been attacked and 35.6% that they had been threatened. Inexperienced therapists were assaulted more often than those with experience and female therapists were assaulted proportionately less than their male colleagues. The ability of these therapists to predict assaultive behaviour seemed very poor: in only 16 of 187 cases were therapists able to predict the confrontation. The actual setting seemed to have little relationship to the threat or assault. 33% of incidents took place in an inpatient setting, 26% in an outpatient context and 21% in private practice.

Private practitioners however seem somewhat less at risk. A survey of 300 psychologists in private practice (Shick–Tryon, 1986) revealed that 81% had experienced attack, abuse or harassment from clients, with verbal abuse being the most common. However, 12% of these 300 therapists had been physically attacked, compared to 24% of a further 250 therapists from other work settings. This difference most likely reflects a screening process within private practice settings that may tend to exclude from therapy more 'difficult' people.

A recent US survey by Schultz (1987), sampled 150 randomly selected social service workers in the one state, from a wide variety of service settings. These ranged from services for children and adolescents, the elderly and handicapped, to correctional settings, and mental health and emergency room services.

83 completed questionnaires indicated an experience of violence. Survey results showed that violence by service recipients had occurred in the following settings (high to low incidence): correctional settings, health/mental health services and handicapped services.

Of the health/mental health personnel surveyed, 3% reported that they had been shot at and 25% of correctional service workers that they had been attacked with knives.

Dubin, Wilson and Mercer (1988) undertook one of the few recent surveys looking at assault against psychiatrists in the outpatient, community-based setting. They surveyed 3,800 psychiatrists from the east coast of the U.S asking them if they were community based and to as whether they had been assaulted on the job. From 91 replies, 32 of them reported serious assaults against themselves with guns or knives and the remaining 59 less serious assaults. There did not appear to be any significant relationship between the patient's diagnosis and the type of assaults. 36% of the assaults were committed by patients who had been in treatment for over a year.

Research in Australia

A number of recent deaths—from shooting, in one incident in Melbourne, Australia—has focused national attention on the possibility of violence occurring in the workplace. This event, and a broader concern with the apparent increase in violence generally in Australian society, has led both State and Federal governments to undertake major investigations into the causes, effects and resolution of violence.

One aspect of these studies has been an inquiry into violence in the workplace. In the Australian context, little research has been undertaken until recently on violence against Human Service Workers while they are undertaking work-related duties (Bowie 1988b).

One major published study was conducted by the Royal Australian Nurses' Federation (Holden 1985). This 1984 survey sampled 310 nurses from all levels of the nursing hierarchy in 17 metropolitan hospitals, 4 country hospitals and 3 community health centres.

Results showed that 85.8% (266 nurses) had been aggressed against by patients; 41.9% (130 nurses) were aggressed against by visitors and 30.9% (96 nurses) reported verbal abuse by co-workers. 43% of respondents stated that they had been abused on 1– 4 occasions in the last 12 months and 15.8% of respondents more than 25 times in the same period. This latter group tended to work in accident and emergency rooms. Only twelve nurses did not report any form of aggression from patients, visitors, co-workers or others.

In a different human service area, Link (1987) surveyed 97 court sheriff's officers in NSW about their experiences of aggression and violence on the job, both in the city and the country.

56% of officers stated that they had been physically assaulted on the job, 21 of them more than three times. 99% had been verbally abused and 47% had death threats made against them in the field or in their offices. 37% had been threatened with a firearm and 80% stated that life threatening incidents had occurred while undertaking their official duties.

73% of these officers felt that the incidents of physical and verbal abuse were increasing in their work situation.

A smaller survey by Bowie (1987) of workers in a Federal social service agency sampled 51 workers from all sections of 2 inner city offices. In this sample, 17.6% had been physically assaulted on the job at some time during their working career. Of this number 3.9% had been assaulted more than two years ago and 13.7% had been attacked physically during the last two years.

While the small sample size can give only indications of trends, it can be noted that some quite senior staff had been assaulted; one worker had been assaulted 12 times, although most had been attacked only once or twice. The ages of staff assaulted ranged from the early twenties to the early forties with a slightly larger number of males being attacked. The survey, however, gives no information about staff who have been assaulted and left the agency in the last two years or those assaulted staff who did not reply to the questionnaire.

Another recent study, (Field 1988) surveyed 880 ambulance officers in the Sydney Central District Ambulance service as regards their experience of assault on the job. 324 survey forms (37%) were returned, reporting 511 assaults against 152 male officers and 18 female officers, with some officers assaulted more than once.

From these replies Field calculates that there is a 22.8% chance that any one officer will be attacked on the job during any one year. Each male officer can, on average, expect to be assaulted every 4 years and 6 months of service and then again within 2 years if previously assaulted. Female officers can expect their first attack around 2 years and 1 month and subsequent assaults after only one year and one month.

The average age of the officers assaulted was 33 years, with 301 of their attackers being under thirty and 182, thirty or over. 47.5% of officers were attacked with fists, 20.1% were kicked and 19.1% were assaulted with other objects apart from knives (8.3%) or firearms (5%).

As would be expected in such incidents whether physical damage is caused or not, there are other 'costs' to the workers involved.

The High Cost of Caring.

Violence leaves not only physical scars but may also have a large emotional impact on workers in a variety of ways. Addiction, suicide, burnout and depression may all be responses by workers feeling trapped in a violence prone work situation. However it should be noted that the above emotional and behavioural responses are not related to the impact of violence and aggression alone upon workers, but to the interaction of a number of stressors.

McCue (1982) gives some idea of the personal cost of caring with one group of human service workers, physicians. He quotes research indicating that the suicide rate of this professional group is two to three times that of the general population and drug addiction at least thirty times that of non-physicians.

An Australian study by Hayes and Fisher (1987) surveyed 1109, mainly NSW medical practitioners, comprising 688 obstetricians/gynaecologists and 502 general practitioners. They investigated the factors in the working lives of doctors which may be related to burnout; the effect of aggression and violence upon the doctors was not directly examined. The question of definition of burnout is left to be examined later in this book.

From their survey they rated 24.7% of obstetricians/gynaecologists and 24.4% of general practitioners in the low burnout category, 61.2% obstetricians/gynaecologists and 66.5% general practitioners as falling into the medium burnout category and 14.2% obstetricians/gynaecologists and 13.4% general practitioners in the high burnout category.

With respect to depression the same sample group reported feeling depressed with the following frequency:

All the time	2.3%
More than three times daily	1.6%
Once or twice daily	0.8%
Every few days	11.6%
Once a week	20.9%
Rarely or never	58.9%
Don't know	3.9%

In the obstetrician/gynaecologist sample, 38.9% reported feeling depressed once a week or more and 46.8% of general practitioners reported the same feelings.

Similar, if somewhat less dramatic, trends might be expected amongst other groups of carers exposed to work stressors equivalent to those faced by doctors.

A study of 274 social workers in the USA (King 1987) identified 10% of them as alcoholics and a further 20% as problem drinkers. Other research has also shown higher than normal rates of suicide in a small sample of New York social workers (Dubrow 1988). Gaskin (1986) quotes figures of an estimated 10% of health professionals as being drug-dependent.

Any in-depth, comparative information on the effects of work stress across a range of types of Human Service Workers is hard to find (Bowie 1982). Any such research is hindered by what McCue calls a 'conspiracy of silence' in which trained Human Service Workers are reluctant to acknowledge any difficulties in coping emotionally or with the day to day realities of the work situation.

Possible Reasons for Increasing Violence in the Workplace

As has been indicated in the above discussion, the research tends to indicate a high number of violent incidents against Human Service Workers. Further, there would appear to be a number of developments in the human services which would support an hypothesised increase in assaults against workers. Weiner & Crosby (1986) provide some reasons for a possible increase in violence in a variety of health, welfare and community services:

- In children's services successful fostering and placement arrangements may leave only the more acting out children in residential care;

- Changes in the mental health act make it more difficult to gain admission for, or have scheduled, people with personality disorders who may create problems for hostels and day centre staff;

- The move toward deinstitutionalisation means discharging into the community patients who have a variety of problems needing ongoing care. Community-based programs may lack resources, the skilled staff and support available in hospitals to manage aggressive patients.

- The current unemployment situation may mean that the more capable developmentally disabled people are forced to remain in sheltered workshops and hostels and become frustrated with those less able around them and with the loss of outside opportunities and autonomy.

- The shift in aged accommodation/hostels is towards an older, but fitter, often mentally confused clientele, who sometimes act aggressively.

- Human Service Workers, teachers and police are required to play an increased investigatory role in a variety of welfare areas, especially in regard to marital violence and child abuse. Workers may face aggression from those they are called to investigate or report.

- During difficult economic times, services to those in need are reduced, raising their frustrations, anxieties and anger. Though agencies have less resources, the impact of their decisions upon disadvantaged service users have assumed greater importance for them.

Given the emerging data summarised above, it would appear that violence against people helpers is a significant issue within the human service professions.

However, any conclusions drawn from this apparent trend towards increasing violence needs to be tempered with a number of other considerations:

- There is no agreed definition of violence, and it is often used in a variety of ways. Violence can include verbal as well as physical injury.

- Is there just a greater awareness of violence through the media and reporting processes rather than actual increases in violence?

- Human Service Workers are often reluctant to record incidents of violence against themselves, and thus, incidence rates may be underestimated.

- Some agencies have no requirement to process and record violent incidents.

- What is the relationship of societal change cycles such as financial hardship, unemployment and family breakdown to the rise and fall of violence ?

These considerations noted above may be partly answered by now looking at some current theories about the causes of violence.

The Causes of Violence

Expert opinion has differed over the years as to whether aggression and violence are innate, instinctual reactions or socially learned behaviour.

Identifying the causes of violence is a difficult, sometimes impossible task, especially for a worker having to deal with the current or end results of violent behaviour.

However, some understanding of the theories of violent behaviour may add further insight to the worker's observations of clients' apparent random or unexplained violence.

An important distinction that can initially be made here is between instrumental or expressive violence. Instrumental violence is seen as violence used to force a person to do something or to stop them doing it. Expressive violence expresses feelings such as fear, confusion, anger, rage or loss of face. A particular violent episode can be a mixture of both or emphasise just one type.

Horwell (1985) attempts to outline a number of theories relevant to an understanding of violence. He is careful to note that, though these theories have something to add to the prediction and control of violence, just because a factor has been linked to violence does not necessarily mean it causes it. Siann (1985) offers a more detailed analysis of the major theories of aggression and violence.

These theories Horwell divides into: Intra-individual theories, Social Psychological theories and Sociocultural theories.

Intra-individual Theories

These theories see aggression as arising from within the individual in the following possible ways;

- **Psychopathology**
  This type of explanation would see violence as coming from individual psychopathology. While the incidence of violence by psychologically disturbed people is below the incidence of the general public, a small proportion of people with certain types of emotional disorders may carry out violent acts. Such disorders may include some types of schizophrenia, acute functional psychosis and so called psychopathic personalities.

- **Alcohol and Drug Induced Aggression**
  Such theories would see violent behaviour as accompanying the abuse of drugs and alcohol.

- **Genetic, Biological or Instinctual Theories**
  Here, violence is seen as due to some inherited biological factor or physical impairment.

- **Excitation–Transfer Theory**
  This theory underlines the possible influence of emotions such as fear, anxiety, sexual excitement, vigorous exercise or an over-stimulating environment, as factors related to violence.

Social Psychological Theories

Here violence and aggression are seen as arising from the effects of social interactions in the following ways:

- **Social Learning Theory**
  This theory suggests that people learn violent behaviour through peers, the family or the media. Such behaviour is learnt through observation, participation or fantasy around violent situations and reinforced by a variety of rewards and avoidance of punishment.

- **Frustration Aggression Theory**
  This subset of Learning theory would see violence as arising from frustration where violence leads to a diminishing of the original frustration.

- **Self Attitude Theory**
  This theory would suggest that some people may use violence as a way of boosting self esteem, for example, through the attention gained by attacking prominent public figures.

- **Boredom and Thrill Seeking**
  Violence may be seen here as an attempt to inject some excitement into a boring life or as a response to a dare.

- **Symbolic Interaction Theory**
  This theory would see peoples' motivation for life as coming from the concepts, meanings and expectations they give to themselves and their social environment. Where people see themselves as being aggressive by nature, in a world where violence is the sanctioned way to succeed, they will be more likely to use violence to 'solve' future problems.

- **Exchange Theory**
  There is the assumption that adequate social interaction involves a balancing of costs and rewards. Where the interaction is not seen as beneficial by one person involved, attempts may be made to redress the imbalance or stop the encounter. These attempts may sometimes involve a resort to violence.

- **Attribution Theory**
  Violence may here be seen as the response of a person who feels that others' actions or intentions against them have a malevolent intention. Violence may take the shape of revenge.

- **De-Individuation Theory**
  Where people are able to lose their sense of individual identity and responsibility, this theory would claim that the likelihood of violence occurring is increased. Soldiers at war or football hooliganism could be examples of this. Also, if potential victims can be categorised as subhuman, deviant, culturally different or part of a hated system, the risk of violence occurring is, again, increased.

Sociocultural Theories

- **Functional Theory**
  The use of violence is seen as performing a certain function in society, perhaps to give new status to a social group or to change or disrupt a relationship or situation. At times, acting out behaviour may be a cry of concern about an existing relationship.

- **Culture of Violence**
  There is an assumption that certain subgroups in society are more violent than others and that they see violence as a legitimate way of gaining certain ends.

- **Conflict Theory**
  This theory holds that conflicts of interest are inevitable amongst different people and that if these differences are not resolved peaceably, violence may occur.

- **Resource Theory**

  This theory assumes that violence may occur where persons lack the resources and power to influence others or a difficult situation. Violence is seen as a way of gaining these needed resources.

- **General Systems Theory**

  General Systems Theory is concerned with the relationships and interactions between the person and their environment. An important aspect is the view that what occurs is not just the sum of the individual actions. That is, with violence, its cause is not seen just in one of the individuals involved, but in both, and their interaction in a particular context.

- **Structural Theory**

  This theory attempts a macro-level analysis of society and the way it is structured in order to show that it is this structuring that causes certain groups to be, or feel, disadvantaged. Such a sense of disadvantage may lead to attempts to change society by violence or the expression of anger and frustration through violent acts.

  This theory incorporates aspects of some of the previous explanations (Frustration, Learning and Subcultural Theories), as does Systems Theory. Horwell claims that it comes as close to an integrated theory of violence as we currently have.

Horwell finally notes that the above theories are oversimplified and all play some part in a comprehensive theory of the cause of violence. Some of these theories tend to be more useful in explaining instrumental violence, others in understanding expressive violence, while others may apply to both.

In practice, however, these theories prove of somewhat limited value in predicting the actual likelihood of violence occurring.

Predicting Violence

Efforts at predicting violence, even in very defined and controlled situations, have not proved to be particularly accurate. Trained mental health personnel, in clinical settings, often have not achieved more than a 50% accuracy in predicting future violent behaviour in light of current information available to them about the potential aggressor (Monahan 1984).

There are a range of factors that are related to aggressive behaviour. Outlined below are some that have been identified from research into actual situations of violence, rather than just being drawn from the more theoretical frameworks suggested by Horwell and others.

Personal Factors

Factors that do seem to bear some relationship to the likelihood of the occurrence of violent actions by a person are:

• A past history of violence;

• Young, single males;

• Low socio-economic status;

• Residential mobility;

• Mental illness.

Besides these demographic and class bound factors there can also be a variety of other personal and attitudinal factors that may lead to violent behaviour. Such aspects can include:

• Unmet physical needs;

• Unmet emotional and self identity needs leading to a desire to prove themselves;

• Displaced anger from past situations projected into the current situation;

- Feelings, attitudes and expectations towards the service organisation.

Each person displays developing aggression in a unique way, however some common signs of impending aggression can include the following;

- Tense and agitated appearance;

- An increase in voice pitch and volume;

- Pupils becoming dilated;

- Change in usual skin colour;

- Angry, withdrawn or brooding behaviour;

- Abrupt responses accompanied by gesticulations;

- Increased physical movement, pacing or banging objects;

- Gathering of potential weapons or allies;

- Acting out behaviour aimed at workers or others;

- Expressed fears of losing control or doing harm to others;

- Evidence of previously seeking help.

However, as Systems Theory would tell us, there is more to a violent situation than just what the other person contributes; there is a dynamic interaction between that person, the staff, the organisation and other external constraints. Some major sources of interaction are outlined below.

Staff Interaction

Workers bring to the job a variety of world views, stresses and needs, which may effect the occurrence of violent situations. These may include:

- Attitudes and satisfaction with the work;

- Feelings, understanding and attitudes towards particular people;

- Previous personal and job history;

- Particular words, incidents or types of people that are hard for that worker to deal with;

- The degree of support available on the job and at home;

- Type and relevance of initial and ongoing training;

- Compounding stress from external events and crises.

Organisational Interaction

The organisation's functioning and setting can also play a major part in effecting the level of violence experienced within its domain. These factors include:

- Type of staff selected and employed and the staffing ratio;

- Induction and ongoing training opportunities;

- Formal and informal power structures amongst staff;

- Extent of mutual decision making available to service users and workers;

- Degree of concern shown both for those receiving help and to staff;

- Type of leadership given;

- Amount of internal (e.g. turnover of staff) and external change (e.g. changed procedures);

- Extent of services and benefits available for recipients;

- How organisational power is experienced by the users through eligibility and discretion requirements and their use or misuse;

- The extent of clear aims, objectives, rules and regulations outlined for those seeking assistance;

- The general physical and emotional climate of the organisation.

Outside Influences

Such factors may effect the efficiency morale and expectations of both service users and staff, these may include:

- Level of finance available to the service;

- Staff shortages or inappropriate workers;

- Type of reputation of the service in the community;

- Public concern and bias over certain issues (e.g. 'dole bludgers', single mothers);

- Worsening financial situation of those in need;

- Involvement and needs of the user's family.

Thus, any attempt to understand, prevent or intervene in violent situations must take into account a whole range of potentially interacting factors, including the service user, worker, organisation and outside factors.

Also, it should be noted that violent behaviour is not static or only of one type, and needs to be understood as also changing and developing over time in response to differing circumstances.

Types and Phases of Violent Behaviour

When the numerous theories on the causes of violence are boiled down, and their essence distilled, there are left a number of pragmatic reasons for violent behaviour by people. Smith (1983) lists the following motives:

- **Fear**
  When people feel they are under attack, or will lose something or someone of value to them, they may respond with expressive violence;

- **Frustration**
  Pent up frustration may lead to rage and destructive violence against people or property of an expressive type;

- **Manipulation**
  In order to force others to give them something they want or to draw attention to themselves some people may become impulsive and violent in an instrumental way;

- **Intimidation**
  Some people may calmly threaten injury to persons or damage to property in order to gain what they want. This may include hostage taking behaviour and other types of instrumental violence.

To these above four reasons for aggressive behaviour could, perhaps, be added those of aggression as a result of pain/illness or brain damage/dysfunction.

Sometimes a knowledge of a person's past history, personality type and social class background may give clues as to which of the above reasons is precipitating a current violent incident. However such knowledge needs to be augmented by a close observation of the current context and the persons behaviour. People acting out from fear, frustration, manipulation or intimidation show some unique characteristics, as outlined below by Smith (1983).

Fear Response

Visual and auditory cues: body tense, ready for fight or flight.
Breathing: irregular, rapid and shallow.
Skin: pale and ashen with the face open eyed and fearful.
Voice: unsteady, whining and pleading.
Personal History: one of withdrawal and victimisation, interspersed by assaultive behaviour.

Frustration Response

Visual and auditory cues: body tense and ready to attack.
Skin: red and purple tones. Face expressing rage.
Breathing: long, deep and heavy.
Voice: loud and aggressive.
Personal History: one of low tolerance for frustration, coupled with episodes of impulsive assault.

Manipulation Response

Visual and auditory cues: often not as clearly observable as the two above, but they do tend to follow a progression.

Firstly, a set of initial, confused demands often in a whining 'victim like' voice. Then, more aggressively expressed accusations and comparisons. Finally, threats and following violent actions.

Personal History: one of poor impulse control and responding with physical attacks when feeling deprived.

Intimidation Response

Visual and auditory cues: neutral and less obvious except for menacing words, voice or threatening stance.

As with manipulation, there is a recognisable progression in words and actions. Firstly, a clear, strongly stated demand. Next, a threat of injury if demands are not met, sometimes accompanied by damage to property. Finally, failure or delay in complying may lead to attempt to injure.

Pain or Impairment Response

Violent responses from pain or brain impairment may be more difficult to interpret and may need a trained observer familiar with that person's particular physical state. Brain impairment that may lead to aggressive behaviour can be the result of complex partial seizures, neurochemical disturbances, metabolic and limbic system imbalances, neoplasms, tumours or other factors.

Aggression arising from such conditions can be sudden and apparently unprovoked and may be unaccompanied by any obvious anger. However, it is essential to recognise that even with aggression due to impairment, factors of personality development, family dynamics, and social situation can play an important additional moderating influence.

The Assault Cycle

Not only is it important for workers to know what is initially motivating a person's violent behaviour, but also they must be able to perceive what level of violence the person has reached. Often they may have to intervene when the violent behaviour is already well under way or when they themselves become the target of an already angered person.

In a situation of escalating violence the aggressor and the victim will display physical, psychological and behavioural responses to the perceived threat that may follow a certain progression. Smith calls this the assault cycle, which is made up of 5 phases:

Phase 1   The triggering event(s)
Phase 2   Escalation
Phase 3   Crisis point
Phase 4   Recovery
Phase 5   Post-crisis depression

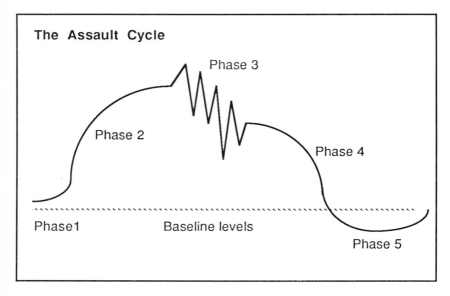

The Assault Cycle

Phase 3

Phase 2

Phase 4

Phase 1   Baseline levels

Phase 5

Figure 1. The Assault Cycle (Adapted from Smith)

- **The Triggering Event**
  This is an occurrence perceived by the individual as a serious threat to them; their perception, not the reality of the event, is the key factor. Triggering events fall into two main types, those of fear and frustration.

  1) Fear inducing events give the person the perception that they are under threat or are to be deprived of something they value.
  2) Frustrating circumstances give the person the idea that their efforts or demands have been useless or ignored.

- **Escalation Phase**
  The person's body and mind prepare to fight. They take a physical stance ready for action and may taunt the perceived threat, if it is a person.

- **Crisis Point**
  The aggressor explodes into violent acts against the threat.

- **Recovery Phase**
  The body relaxes and the mind decreases its vigilance, the confrontation is seen to be over, even if only temporarily.

- **Post-Crisis Depression**
  While the body and mind try to return to a stable base level, the physical and emotional aspects of the crisis reappear in this phase often as fatigue, depression and guilt.

Useful as this concept of an assault cycle is, it must be qualified in a number of ways:

- Each individual is different in the way they experience and express violent behaviour due to a range of personality, history and contextual factors;

- The cycle may not necessarily be followed right through by the aggressor to the post-crisis depression stage. It may be short circuited by intervention at any prior phase, or in the recovery phase further violent behaviour may be triggered off;

- Some personality types do not seem to feel the guilt and depression aspect of the last phase but may be further aroused by the incident.

With these qualifications, this model is still a useful way of examining violent behaviour in order to plan an appropriate response. This model is helpful in incidents not only of physical violence but also in understanding cycles of intense verbal abuse.

Such information about the causes and cycles of violence must then be incorporated into the way workers use their verbal and non-verbal skills to prevent or defuse a violent situation. Such skills are dealt with in the next chapter.

Chapter Three. Crisis Communication Strategies.

Controlling the Situation

In a situation of potential or actual violence there are three main ways of gaining or maintaining control. The first two are interrelated and rely on intellectual and emotional processes (verbal persuasion and reasoning) and social pressures (family, culture, control agents) while the third relies on physical and chemical restraints.

Verbal persuasion is a way of changing a situation through talk that in turn changes the behaviour of those involved. Events that call for fight or flight have passed the persuasion stage. The verbal and social means of control open to workers will be examined here. The verbal techniques outlined below are largely based on those originally suggested by Thompson (1983).

The situation to be controlled is influenced by the problem, those involved and the constraints.

* The problem must be a situation that, actually or potentially, can be influenced by verbal persuasion or by other means available to the worker.

* Those involved must be capable of being influenced by words or other actions.

* The constraints are other persons, events, objects and relationships that are part of the situation.

Types of Persuasion Situations

A persuasion situation can be simple or complex; highly structured or loosely structured.

A simple situation is where only a few elements have to be made to interact, such as a worker facing an aggressive person alone. A complex situation is one where numerous elements interact, for example, where a number of patients on a ward threaten to assault a staff member, encouraged by other patients. The skill in either situation is to recognise the problem, know who is the appropriate 'audience' and what the actual constraints are in the situation.

A highly structured persuasion situation is one in which all the relevant elements are identified and are ready for the tasks to be performed. A loosely structured situation is one lacking control and containing a number of potentially unknown factors.

There can be four main types of persuasion situations: complex highly structured, complex loosely structured, simple highly structured and simple loosely structured.

These are ideal types and many persuasion scenes are of a loosely structured nature.

Control in any situation can be weakened further by complexity and/or disconnectedness of the types below.

- A single situation may have multiple problems;

- Two or more situations may compete for the worker's attention;

- Persons, part of one group, may also be participants in a number of other situations.

A situation in which a worker is involved in will change over time. The worker's aim is to be in control of this change through re-creating a new situation from different, potentially dangerous situations. The worker's aim is to be in control (balance) of the changes, rather than being controlled by them. Note that timing is crucial in all these persuasion encounters which have a limited life, moving from development to decay. Thus, the worker needs to judge what is the appropriate response for the life cycle of that particular situation.

In order to maintain this balance the worker needs to develop the skills to deal with the following types of complex situations that may arise.

Dealing With Complexity

- **Multiple Problems**

  Where there are multiple problems within a single situation the worker's role will be to assess the competing problems and select one as the central focus. Such a decision will be aided by analysing the severity of each problem and the probability of changing this problem by persuasion, rather than force.

  An example of such a situation could be that of a worker going to the aid of a fellow worker who is being threatened by a group of people, some of whom, the first worker knows well.

- **Competing Situations**

  The worker's role here may be to negotiate each situation independently or to create an entirely new situation, dealing with both as part of a larger scene. To do this, the worker must be capable of recognising that there are indeed competing scenes, and then be capable of transforming both into a more controllable, single situation.

  An example of competing situations could be where an aggressor has lit a fire and, by threatening the life of another person, is trying to prevent staff from extinguishing it.

- **Competing Audiences**

  Here the worker needs to take charge of such a complex situation through re-creation. Successful control, or balance, involves the worker in making themselves the primary audience and minimising the effects of the other competing audience.

A situation of competing audiences could be when a worker tries to calm an aggressive person who has also become the focus of hostility of others around them.

Types of Audiences

In a situation of actual or potential violence, a worker may have to deal with people of differing numbers and familiarity to the worker. Such combinations include;

- Single person, known to worker;

- Single person, unknown;

- Single group, known;

- Single group, unknown;

- Multiple groups, known;

- Multiple groups, unknown.

In reality the audience is often a mixture of these groups. A worker's approach must obviously differ according to the particular combination of people that they are facing. However, the worker in all these situations must try continuously to make the 'unknown' the 'known', yet never assume that the 'known' will always remain that way.

When the worker is able to define the individual or groups as having certain characteristics, they are then in a position to make certain decisions about what methods of persuasion to use. A variety of persuasion methods that workers need to be able to use skillfully are outlined below.

Communication and Intervention

There are some basic communication principles of which workers must be aware and practise if they are to handle, in an appropriate fashion, situations of aggression. These major principles, suggested by Everstein & Everstein (1983) are:

- A person cannot AVOID communicating;

- Communication involves content and context factors;

- The message sent is not always the message received.

Communication involves much more than words and even remaining silent can have an effect upon an aggressor through the influence of other, non-verbal cues.

Disagreements can escalate when the context and content of a message are misunderstood and further action is based on this misperception. Disputes about content, the facts, are usually more easily settled than those about context, the person's world view. Disagreements about context arise when one person misperceives or misunderstands what another has said or done. Much of what is considered reality by a worker or the other person is really only the sum total of their own personal set of assumptions.

In attempting to communicate in a crisis situation the worker is faced with trying to get across a message to another who does not necessarily share their same view of reality or life experience. The worker's primary task here is to understand the other's world view and try to communicate to them in a way which is relevant to their view and the current crisis situation.

Most people have a reason for behaving aggressively that makes some sort of sense to them. The worker's role is to try and understand the other's system of logic and, where appropriate, incorporate the others' style of logic into their own communication process.

Obviously crucial to any intervention is the method and means of communication used. Thackery (1987b) provides a useful analysis of the methods and means of communication relevant to aggressive people.

He reminds us that communication is more than words and that it involves the sending of signals through the verbal, paraverbal, kinesic, proxemic and haptic channels, as outlined below.

Verbal channels use words, with both literal and implied meanings, in the process of persuading others.

Verbal Persuasion

Aristotle suggested that persuading others can be done in three ways:

- by appeal to their reason;

- by appeal to their emotions;

- by appeal of our character and personality (persona).

Two other related verbal means of persuasion are:

- appeal to consequences;

- appeal to socio-cultural pressures.

These may be sub-categories of the first three.

The choice of persuasion approaches to take will, as before, be influenced by the situation (context), the problem, constraints and the audience. The worker's perspective and purpose also will guide selection of the appropriate approaches.

Appeal to Reason

Appeals to reason operate at the thinking, rational, level and can involve several approaches.

One approach is through problem solving, in which attempts are made to solve the frustration or problem as perceived by the other person. A second, related approach may be by clarification and re-interpretation of events and information through questioning and advice giving to an agitated or aggressive person.

A third major approach is that of correcting basic errors in their logic, thus leading them to re-interpret events in a less aggressive fashion.

In using reason, a worker needs to know how to correct four basic logical errors that people often make in conflict situations. These four errors of reasoning are as follows:

- **'Either/Or' Fallacy**

   This is the tendency to see only one solution to a problem. The worker's role here may be to point out other unseen alternatives and help find a mutually acceptable, non violent, third way.

- **Faulty Generalisation**

   This includes jumping to conclusions based on inadequate or faulty information. The worker's role may be to get the other person to re-examine the sources of their information and the ways they may be incorrect, (for example, irrelevant, unrepresentative, biased or out of context generalisations).

- **Faulty Causal Generalisation**

   This involves seeing only one cause of the problem and not considering the possibility of several causes. Here the worker's role may be to point out hasty generalisations or incorrect identification and in a calm, reasonable manner encourage the person to think about what they have been saying. The attempt here is to shift the subject's focus from their faulty conclusions to their means of reasoning.

- ***Ad Hominem* Arguments**

   Such types of faulty reasoning involve majoring on personalities rather than on the facts and issues at hand. The worker's role here is to focus the client's attention on the facts and the problems and not on attacking individuals or personality types.

In all appeals to reason, the focus should be aimed at inquiry and clarification, rather than reaction.

Appeal to Emotion

An appeal to emotions is probably the strongest means of persuasion and often must be used indirectly.

Words have two kinds of meanings: their literal (denotative) use and their emotional (connotative) meaning for an individual. Certain words have powerful connotations (feelings and memories) attached to them that can trigger strong emotional reactions in people (eg. dole bludger, bureaucrat, the 'welfare', eligibility).

A word's particular connotations for a person are affected by their senses, beliefs, prejudices and insecurities. Thus, to avoid negative connotations, the worker must choose words that will trigger positive reactions; ones that show an appreciation of the person's culture and avoid culturally and racially biased words that will close down communication. Similarly, a worker must be sensitive to the other's area of insecurity, using words that emphasise strengths rather than weaknesses. Occasionally, these insecurities may be highlighted as a planned strategy to get someone to back off from a proposed course of action. However, such strategies should only be used with great caution.

Use of Ethical Appeal

This refers to the use of the worker's own authority and character or 'persona', or their relationship with the other person, as a means of persuasion.

Right from the beginning, the worker needs to establish their presence on the scene in a persuasive, though often low-key, fashion. Throughout the evolution of the situation, a fair, just and reasonable persona must be presented that will maintain, wherever possible, the worker's credit and goodwill for the future. Thus, in selecting an appropriate role and the voice to match it, the worker can use their voice for appeals based on reason, emotion and persona.

Appeal to Consequences

This method of persuasion is a particular application of methods one and two in which the probable end results of certain behaviour are pointed out to the person. Wherever possible, the consequences should be framed in a positive light rather than from a negative, punishing perspective, pointing out how they will benefit from good and co-operative behaviour.

Appeals to Socio-Cultural Pressures

These may include appeals to family honour or face, cultural identity, peer pressure, institutional expectations or societal norms for behaviour.

Non-Verbal Persuasion

Alongside of these types of verbal persuasion there are also non-verbal means or 'channels' of communication—the para-verbal, the kinesic, the proxemic and the haptic—that must be congruent with the verbal message.

Paraverbal means of communication are utterances, sounds and pauses, as well as tone, inflection and volume, but not actual words.

Kinesic channels include body posture, stance, eye contact, facial expressions, movements and gestures. Closely related to these are cues like physical appearance and clothing style.

Proxemics relate to use and structuring of space with objects and people. Private space and territoriality are important factors to be taken into account. Intrusion on perceived private space by a worker, even in apparently public areas, may lead to aggressive responses by an other.

Haptic channels involve the use of touch and how it is used.

Normally in communication, all these different channels must be used in an integrated fashion and not distract from each other, or negate the message of any other channel. On some occasions paradox as a chosen method of communication may be carefully used where conflicting or unexpected messages are purposely used to intervene. However, paradox should be used only sparingly and as a chosen strategy.

Thackery goes on to suggest that the above five communication channels can be seen to occupy a hierarchy, with the further down the hierarchy the channel used, the more simple and less conscious is the message conveyed.

Also, during times of increasing stress, the communication capacity of the channels is lost from the top down; that is, with increasing distress both the other's and the worker's verbal ability and message perception may be replaced by non-verbal responses and needs. As the situation is resolved, the reverse may occur, with movement up towards the more verbal, conscious channels.

This communication hierarchy can also be related to Smith's assault cycle, especially in its first three stages (trigger, escalation and crisis). In each of these stages a different type and means of communication is called for, through a different but congruent blending of the channels.

Thus, the worker's role in their communication is to choose the appropriate mix of channels, at the right time, in order to communicate most meaningfully to the person at their current level of distress.

Thackery gives some further helpful clues in choosing the right mix of channels.

Verbal Channels

In an escalating situation the worker should use simple, non abstract words in a clear and concrete way. Smith refers to 'the rule of five', which states that, during a crisis intervention situation, sentences used should be limited to no more than five words, and the words used be limited to five letters or less.

Two particularly useful verbal techniques for defusing situations are those of By-pass and Broken Record.

By-pass involves the worker acknowledging the aggressor's statements, but without reflecting emotion, in a non-defensive manner and without responding to any abusive or insulting language. The worker then goes on and says, in a controlled manner, what they wish to say. It is difficult for a person to maintain a feeling of high emotion for long when there is no emotion being returned for their own anger to feed on. To be effective, by-pass must never sound flippant or like a 'put down' or as an attempt to avoid the issue.

The Broken Record technique is simply that of repeating the basic message that needs to be communicated until the aggressor responds to the message. The reason for doing this is to get the other person's mind operating back at a reasonably rational level again. At first, the person's conscious mind may not register the message but it will lodge in the subconscious and, with repetition, it may move across into the conscious level, especially where used in conjunction with the By-pass technique. The repetition may need to be discontinued if it causes further agitation in the aggressor.

By-pass aims to set the emotions aside in order to allow the Broken Record technique to have its effect. When such techniques are used workers must show great self control and not become upset or diverted from their task. Also their tone of voice and body language must match their spoken message or these techniques could backfire and make the situation worse.

Paraverbal Channels

Non-verbal Level

A calming or limit-setting style of voice tone, speed and inflection should be chosen to defuse situations of expressive or instrumental violence. Speaking in a slow, controlled fashion, without raising the voice is best. At times lowering the volume of the voice may be an appropriate response.

Kinesic Level (Body Posture and Motion)

Eye contact, facial expression and posture must present a non-aggressive appearance. In instances of manipulation or intimidation a stance indicating control will be used and in others, such as fear or frustration, one of alliance and support. Such stances will be detailed later. Eye contact must be appropriate to the person, their culture and the situation.

Proxemic Level (Personal Space)

The other person should be allowed to define what is comfortable personal space for them in a public and private situation. Research has indicated that people with a history of violence tend to need a larger personal space zone than non-violent individuals (Hildreth, Derogatis and McCusker 1971). Both the worker and the other person should not feel trapped or cornered in a contact situation. This trapped feeling can be both a physical and emotional reality.

Haptic Level (Touch)

Touch may be used mainly with fearful people, sometimes at the beginning of a possible assault cycle and especially at the end of a cycle in the depression phase.

Touch can have a powerful calming and healing effect, however, when applied at the wrong stage of the assault cycle it can be misinterpreted by the other person as a threat. Those people with some sort of delusional system or victims of previous physical or sexual abuse may react negatively to any attempt at close physical contact.

Non-Verbal Communication Under Stress

The greatest resource in any confrontation is the worker's mind willing the body to be outwardly calm and then inwardly so. In this calm or centred state the worker is better able to assess the emotional balance of the aggressor or signs of impending attack, as well as being able to analyse the environment in which the violence occurs. Self control must come before situation control.

In a situation of confrontation it is normal for a worker to tense their muscles ready for a response as the situation develops, however this may signal to the aggressor, staff fear or readiness to attack. Also, in such a state of tension both sides of a muscle group are tightened, meaning one set must be released if an urgent response is needed, thus slowing the crucial action, such as blocking or running.

Under stress the worker's breathing may also become shallower, cutting off much needed oxygen to the brain. At the same time, the pitch and volume of the voice may change. This is the opposite of what is needed in crisis, that is, to think rationally and speak clearly and confidently.

Of obvious key importance under such circumstances is the worker's use and control of their breathing. Maintaining a focus on the breathing can give the worker something to concentrate on prior to, and during, a crisis as well as keeping up the much needed oxygen flow to the brain.

Therefore, the worker must consciously question and control what is happening physically and talk themselves into a state of calmness. With this 'self talk' the worker needs constantly to be monitoring crucial aspects of their non-verbal behaviour; stance and posture, distance, eye contact, breathing, voice modulation and clarity.

These self talk questions may include some of the following:

> 'Am I relaxed and in control of myself?'
> 'How can I intervene without drawing undue attention to the situation?'
> 'Am I using my voice in a calm, controlled and confident manner?'
> 'Are my non-verbal cues matching my spoken message?'
> 'How can I avoid being trapped or cornering the other person?'
> 'Am I able to resolve this problem or should I seek help?'

Alongside this self monitoring, the worker must then behave in certain ways and use verbal and non-verbal approaches appropriate to the situation, as outlined below.

Basic Intervention Strategies

Some useful actions to use are as follows:

- Whenever possible, have the permission of those involved to enter a crisis situation;

- Intervene as soon as possible for maximum impact and potential change;

- Use isolation or distraction where appropriate. If necessary remove any disruptive stimulus or individual;

- Respect the other person's private physical and emotional space. Do whatever is necessary to avoid being seen as a threat or intruding;

- Avoid cornering the aggressor. There are four types of cornering: angular cornering (trapping in the angle of two walls); exit cornering (blocking the means of escape); contact cornering (holding another to prevent them leaving); and psychological or verbal cornering of a win–lose type;

- Concentrate on building relationships. In high stress situations people begin quickly to structure set rules for the relationship and the worker needs to be directing the development of this relationship while help is being given. The aim is to develop a strong bond between the person in crisis and the worker, in order to make it possible for the other person to be part of the resolution process.

Problems may often arise when the worker misunderstands how the person wishes or needs to define the relationship. Conflicts occur when one person attempts to treat the other as an equal while the other wishes to be treated as superior or inferior or tries to treat the other in the relationship in a way they do not want or need.

Thus the worker must be sensitive and flexible as to how the other wants the relationship to be, as revealed through their verbal and non-verbal cues.

An example here could be the use of a person's name as they wish it; not too formal or too intimate, but what makes them feel comfortable.

Communication for Change

The above interventions also need to be supported by some of the verbal strategies outlined below:

- Early on, get the person to agree to something, either in word or action, thus building the first small step of co-operation.

- Incorporate, wherever possible, the aggressor's own worldview into the design of the helping process by re-framing parts of their perceptions. This involves accepting and reinterpreting their hostile actions in a more positive light; seeking points of similarity rather than differences and enlisting their help as allies rather than as enemies. However, this must be carefully done so as not to reinforce delusional beliefs or totally negative worldviews.

- Comment on the other person's behaviour, not on their apparent motivation. Avoid the impression of trying to read their mind or of judging their intent. Give the person psychological room to explain or deny feelings attached to their actions.

- Deal with the 'here and now' rather than on issues of the past. Be aware that people in crisis often cling strongly to past, concrete ways of thinking and coping.

- Keep explanations or instructions simple, avoid complex or loaded words such as 'any', 'never' or 'all', that are often used in black or white, exaggerated statements.

- Reassure, calm and support the aggressor, stating that the worker is there to help them maintain control of themself. Encourage the other person to understand and accept the responsibility for controlling their own behaviour.

- Keep requests short, direct and non-condescending. Don't speak as a parent to a child, risking projection and further anger.

- When asking questions, avoid casting doubt on the other person's ability to perform a task, but rather their willingness to do so. The former can be seen patronising or insulting and may further damage the person's low self esteem.

- Avoid making promises or guarantees that cannot be kept or that are beyond your control. Talk about what is known, don't attempt to predict future outcomes or events. If the guarantees fail or the predictions don't happen, the person in crisis will be further traumatised and the helper's credibility damaged.

- Wherever possible offer the person in crisis a face saving alternative or a way out, as they are often feeling trapped or confused. Offer the 'illusion' of alternatives where there is a seemingly free choice amongst a number of alternatives, but with the same end result, the de-escalation of the situation.

- Where limits need to be set for the person in crisis they should be framed in a positive, non superior–inferior way, conveying the worker's desire to help but not to allow manipulation.

  Any limits that are set should be reasonable and easily understood. Check that the aggressor understands the limits and reinforce the benefits for them in complying with them.

Limit setting can either be in the form of a direct command or request or in an indirect form in which the person is given a series of choices among acceptable behaviour alternatives. The worker must decide whether the direct or indirect approach to setting limits is the most appropriate to the person and context at that time.

- Don't overreact when a person threatens to harm another. Such overreaction can reinforce further aggressive behaviour and be used to manipulate the worker. Try to take the focus off the threatened person and onto what the aggressor wants and needs.

- Use praise carefully, embedding it between neutral statements, thus complementing the person in crisis without totally rejecting or downplaying their current, negative self image. Avoid trying glibly to cheer up a depressed person, this may appear not to treat their current view of reality seriously. At the same time give credit to the other person for coping for so long and affirm that they are a person of worth.

- Slow and extend the communication where appropriate. This approach shows that the worker thinks the other is important and worth listening to. It also gives the worker time to listen, analyse and appropriately respond.

- Where the situation has not yet reached the crisis state the situation may be defused by the worker seeking further information from the person in order to help them. Such a request may divert the person's attention away from expressing anger into clarifying their side of the situation. However the worker must be alert for any signs of irritation at such requests.

- The use of paradox or distraction may sometimes be appropriate, for example, asking for a drink of water, commenting on the smell of gas or faking a dizzy spell. These actions may give the worker opportunity to redirect the encounter in a more positive direction.

- Above all, the worker should let the other person know that they have heard what the problem is, and acknowledge it as a problem, and then let them talk about what has made them upset or angry. The worker should aim to clarify as much as possible what is motivating the person's aggressive behaviour

These are basic guidelines for intervention in most crisis situations but there are some additional points that need to be born in mind when intervening in the potentially more vulnerable community or home-based setting.

Community-Based Settings

The above strategies are generally applicable to a variety of settings. The pace and type of intervention may be slower and different on the other person's territory compared with that in a worker's office or other work situation. If visiting a person with a history of violence at their home, special precautions may need to be taken. Everstein & Everstein suggest the following strategies for workers going on home visits:

- Gather relevant information ahead of time about the person and the situation you are visiting;

- Operate according to a plan to eliminate wasted time and additional visits;

- Let others know where you are going and the expected time of your return;

- Where appropriate ask for police support and do not go alone, especially at night;

- Park a short distance from the home and walk quietly towards the scene;

- Listen for sounds of disturbance or anything unusual. Don't assume that if you can't see or hear someone that you aren't being observed;

- Stand back a little from the door and not directly in front of it. This will give the other person space and the worker will present less of a target and also have room to move if needed;

- Identify yourself and do not enter without being invited;

- On entering, identify yourself again and observe the state of house. Note any possible avenues of escape if needed;

- Respect the other person's personal boundaries and private areas;

- Choose an appropriate place for meeting, avoid bedrooms, kitchens or a favourite chair. Stay clear of potential weapons;

- Sit down at the same time as the other person and avoid, where possible, interviewing in a cluttered or noisy environment;

- If there is more than one worker or a number of people that you are visiting, decide whether a group or individual approach, or both, over time, is needed;

- Clearly demonstrate your interest in the person and your desire to help them clarify their problem and, where possible, find a solution to it;

- Try to end the visit on a positive note;

- Document as soon as possible any necessary information gathered on the visit;

Alongside of these procedural and verbal skills there is also a need for workers to be familiar and practised in the use of physical intervention skills. These skills are examined in the next chapter.

Chapter Four. Principles of Physical Intervention

Basic Physical Intervention Strategies.

Sound judgment must continually be used when implementing both psychological and physical method of intervention. There is no one physical response to violence for all situations and each worker must apply learnt principles to what they observe in the situation around them. A worker's age, physical fitness, build, self confidence and experience may influence the particular physical intervention techniques they choose.

The approach suggested here is a 'soft' one, based largely on the approach outlined by Thackery (1987b). It tries to avoid any infliction of pain or the use of unnecessary force by the worker against an aggressor. For some workers in a care or control situation such approaches may seem unrealistic or too soft for the realities of their workplace. They may wish to modify these approaches or learn advanced control techniques relevant to their own job.

Methods of restraining or controlling violent individuals will not be addressed here, as such advanced skills need to be learnt in a real life training situation and are beyond the scope of this book.

A worker needs to be prepared for physical intervention in three ways as outlined by Thackery:

- psychologically

- perceptually

- physically

- **Psychological** preparedness involves the worker having their feelings under control and being able to judge their limitations in the situation; should they stay, leave or ask for help?

Such preparedness also involves acknowledging that an appropriate response may still be costly to them physically and emotionally, thus helping the worker to avoid reacting out of desperation.

Workers under attack will at least feel fear and then possibly anger. Both emotions need to be recognised and controlled. Both can reduce the speed of self-defence responses and block clear-minded thinking that is needed for persuasion or finding ways of escape. Responses fueled by anger can lead to overreaction and the use of unnecessary, destructive force, while fearful responses may lead to panic or 'freezing'.

- **Perceptual** preparedness involves the worker being able to anticipate the aggressor's actions and reactions and use them as part of the intervention strategy, or as a means of escape or diversion.

- **Physical** preparedness involves a number of practices and responses which need to be learnt and performed in sequence at the appropriate times.

As previously mentioned, control and use of breathing must be a priority for any worker anticipating or actually in, a situation of conflict. Breathing is the easiest physiological system to control and if a worker can gain control quickly and consciously over their breathing response they can then proceed to master more ably other fear and panic responses.

The very act of focusing upon the breathing first can help block out some initial feelings that might ordinarily overwhelm the worker when faced with potential violence. Controlled breathing should also be used during the actual conflict to maintain the worker at their physical and mental peak, and again at its conclusion as the worker recovers from the impact of the event.

Control of breathing need not be a complicated process and may simply involve taking a number of deep breaths before entering a conflict situation. There are a number of breathing techniques that can be used or adapted to the needs and preferences of each worker (Mason 1980).

Some other practices involved in physical preparedness are outlined below and are then expanded in the later section on evasive self defence:

A   Danger and Safety Zones

An important practice is to avoid standing in the danger zone. There are three zones surrounding an aggressor:

- The distant safety zone, where the worker cannot be reached by a punch or kick;

- The danger zone, where a worker can be struck forcibly;

- The close safety zone, where the aggressor cannot effectively deliver a major blow to a worker with their knee, elbow or head (see figure 2).

Depending on the tactics used, the worker may choose to remain in either of the safety zones while avoiding, entering or remaining within the danger zone.

As an aggressor can move most forcefully straight ahead, less easily to the side and only with difficulty backwards, a worker should avoid the front of an attacker, choosing where possible the side or back positions. The worker should remain out of the danger zone and slightly to one side of the aggressor, rather than directly in front of them. Avoid crowding, sudden movements or threatening gestures.

Normally a worker should stand an arm's length (the aggressor's arm's length) plus a further hand's length back from the aggressor. This puts the worker outside of the other person's reach or kick and avoids impinging on their personal space, while positioning the worker far enough away not to give the impression of their backing away in fear. Remember that an assailant can reach further with a kick than a punch.

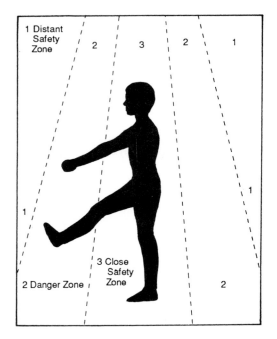

Figure 2. Danger and Safety Zones

B   Posture

In a situation that has not yet become hostile a worker's arms should not be folded or crossed giving a hostile or defensive message, but should be kept at the side of the body with fists unclenched, not pointing, gesturing or using threatening actions (picture 1).

A non-threatening, protective posture is assumed when the worker anticipates an attempt to punch, strike or kick them.

This stance aims to protect the worker without threatening the person or signalling worker anxiety.

There are a number of variations of the non-threatening, protected posture and one stance is shown in picture 2. In these postures the worker keeps a sideways, angled stance to the aggressor while having the hands in a 'natural' position but ready for rapid self-protective movement.

At the same time the staff member needs to judge the aggressor's dominant side, whether they are right or left handed. The worker should stand slightly off centre to the aggressor's weaker side, as a blow is most likely to come from the person's dominant hand or foot. Most people are right handed and right footed and wear their watches on their weak sided wrist. Thus in most instances it is 'safer' for the worker to stand at an angle to an aggressor's left side, when it is their weaker, non-dominant side (see figure 3).

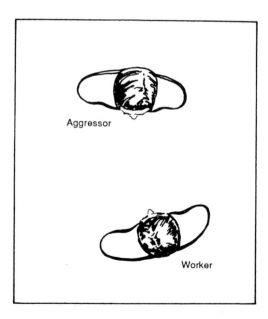

Figure 3. Worker standing at angle to aggressor's non-dominant side.

Picture 1. Open, non-threatening posture with basic balance stance.

Picture 2. Non-threatening protected posture with leaning stance.

C   Appropriate Stance

The majority of injuries to staff from assault occur once they have been knocked down (Moran 1984). It seems that a staff person down on the ground communicates greater vulnerability to an attacker, encouraging further violence. Therefore, it is important for workers to know not only how to stand and remain so, but also what position to take to ensure that any blow does the least amount of damage.

•   Basic Balance Stance

In a situation of verbal violence the worker should stand with feet slightly spread, approximately the same width as the outside of the shoulders. Stance is strongest along an imaginary line drawn through both feet and is weakest perpendicular to that line, that is, through the toes to the heels.

A basic balance should be maintained by keeping the hips directly above and between the feet and with the shoulders directly above the hips. Avoid upsetting this balance by allowing the upper body to sway outside of the feet.

•   Leaning Stance

If the situation becomes more tense, the worker unobtrusively moves their dominant leg slightly to the rear, knee unbent and the other leg slightly forward of the body, bent slightly at the knee. This stance is extremely stable and will minimise the odds of a person being knocked down. (figure 4)

D   Eye Contact

The worker should use eye contact carefully; too much can be interpreted as a challenging gesture. Different cultures have different ideas of what is acceptable eye contact. Glance from time to time at the eyes but also watch the throat at collar button level. This allows awareness of any movement and also allows peripheral vision to pick up any hand or foot movement.

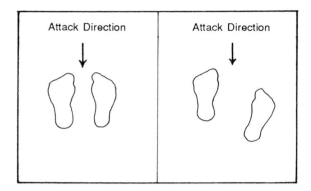

Figure 4. A. Basic balance stance. B. Leaning stance.

E   Protection of Head and Throat

The head is the part of the body most sensitive to blows and the neck is the part most vulnerable to choking. Where possible all vulnerable parts should be turned away from attack and covered.

F   Don't Oppose Force

The worker should not directly oppose the force of an attacker, but should attempt to move their body away from an attack unless they have been captured. If captured, a worker should move their body weight in the direction of the capture.

G   Pivotal Moving

When moving out of harm's way, the worker should attempt to move in a circular pivoting motion (see figure 5).

If it is necessary to keep moving near the attacker without leaving the situation, use the 'boxer's shuffle', standing on the balls of the feet and alternatively moving the feet in towards the centre of the body and then out again.

H   Deflection

Sometimes it may be necessary to deflect a blow with a non-vital body part or an object, with the deflection being used at an angle rather than directly against the attack.

I   Controlling the Aggressor's Hands

When held, the worker must establish control over the grabbing hands as a first priority in order to minimise damage to the captured section of the body.

J   Induce Weak Position

When held, the worker should attempt to position the attacker in a relatively weak position. The thumb is the weakest part of the grip and unlike the other fingers it is not suited to grabbing. Often, in attempting to gain release from a grab, the best procedure is to work on the thumb, and not the other fingers.

K   Apply Torque

Torque is a twisting and rotating action that is difficult to control and is used as part of many escape techniques, such as releasing grabs or chokes.

L   Use Energy Cycle

The worker should aim to be at their peak of energy when the attacker is tiring and try to act at the time of the aggressor's minimal power.

M   Use Weight Leverage

The worker should aim to use their body weight and that of the attacker to their own advantage and to tire an attacker. Some release can be accomplished by wedging (gradually prising apart) or using leverage at a more vulnerable part of the grip.

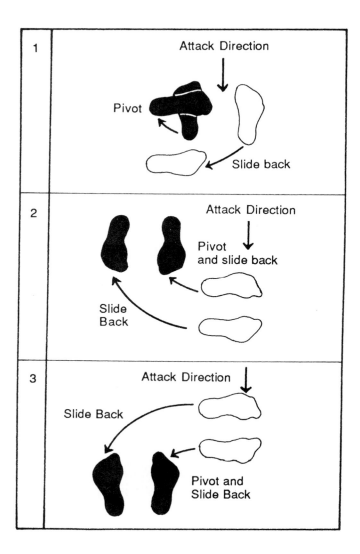

Figure 5. Three variations of pivoting movements (overhead view):
(1) Pivoting on either foot away from frontal attack off to one side;
(2) Pivoting on closest foot from a sideways position;
(3) Pivoting on furthest foot from sideways position.

Evasive Self-Defence

Here are outlined in more detail some basic physical techniques for self preservation. They illustrate ways in which workers can avoid harm to themselves and escape from physically dangerous holds or situations. They are not intended as means of control or punishment for violent people. Containment and control of violently acting out individuals is a specialist field beyond the scope of this book and only should be taught by experts in a controlled training situation.

Possible attacks are of two major types:

- Strikes and punches;

- Grabs and holds.

The general defence against strikes and punches is deflection and/or blocking. The general defence against grabs and holds is control of the aggressor's grabbing hands.

Defences Against Strikes, Punches and Other Attacks

Depending on the worker's assessment of the situation they may decide to stay far enough away as to avoid physical contact, or alternatively may move in close so as to make a punch or kick ineffective.

In close contact the worker may use a 'checking block' (picture 3) which can smother or deflect an attack. Checking blocks can also be used in a preventative way to stop an attack before it begins (picture 4).

When a worker is not able to move out of the danger zone they must be able to block or deflect an attack with their arms, legs or any appropriate object (eg chair, book, pillow or jacket). Under actual attack the worker should have their hands protecting their head, throat and chest. Many blocking motions start with at least one hand up near the face (picture 5), so as to protect the worker's head and, if necessary to be moved rapidly downwards to protect the body.

Picture 3. In order to stop an impending punch, the worker enters the close safety zone and prevents a clear punch with a checking block.

Picture 4. The worker using a checking block to prevent an attack.

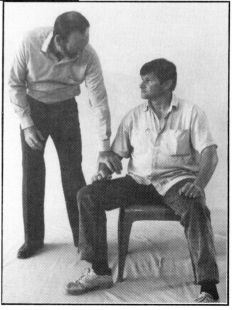

Picture 5. Worker protecting the head, throat and chest

Examples of deflecting or blocking are shown in pictures 6–11

In picture 6 the worker moves their hands from the non-threatening protected position to shield the head and throat while moving sideways.

In picture 7 the worker pivots to one side, away from the attacker, and blocks the high punch, pushing it away rather than directly absorbing the attacker's force head on. Where the worker is not able to avoid the force of the blow, they may be able to absorb most of the blow aimed at the head and throat by protective use of the hands and arms (picture 8).

If the blows are aimed at the abdomen the worker can bring both arms quickly down to protect the midsection and thighs (picture 9).

Picture 6. The worker protects their head while moving sideways and blocks the high punch.

Picture 7. The worker pivots to one side while blocking the high punch.

Picture 8. Using worker's arms and hands to protect the head and throat.

Picture 9. Using the arms to protect the midsection.

Picture 10. Blocking blows to the lower body by protective use of the legs.

Picture 11. Worker protects self while on the ground by absorbing kicks with the soles of their feet.

Where there are low kicks aimed at the groin or abdomen they may be blocked and absorbed by the shins and lower leg (picture 10).

If the worker is on the ground they may protect themselves from kicks by pivoting on their buttocks, keeping their feet towards an attacker and absorbing any kicks with the soles of their shoes (picture 11).

Where the worker is being attacked with an object (eg knife, club, chair) they may use another common object, such a book or handbag, as a defensive shield. Such objects are to be used as blocking instruments and not as means of retaliation.

Defence Against Grabs and Holds

The worker should avoid remaining in the danger zone. If this is not possible the worker can attempt to pivot and deflect an attacker's attempted grab or push (pictures 12 and 13).

Where the worker has actually been grabbed by the wrist/s, they may decide not to resist, but to attempt other verbal, reasoning and non-verbal intervention methods.

Where the worker feels it necessary to remove the wrist hold, a number of releases can be used that direct the worker's efforts at the weakest point of the attacker's grip, their thumbs.

Picture 12. Worker ready to pivot out of the way of an attacker's attempted grab.

Picture 13. Worker deflecting an attempted grab or push.

In all these releases the worker maximises their strength by bending their arm at the elbow and acting swiftly before the aggressor has time to act or resist the release. These releases are illustrated in pictures 14 to 19.

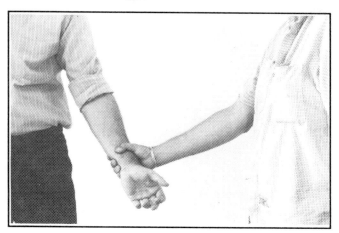

Picture 14.

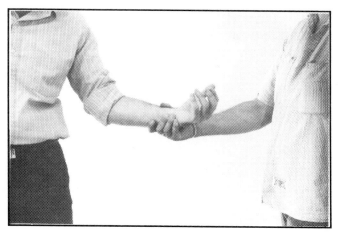

Picture 15.

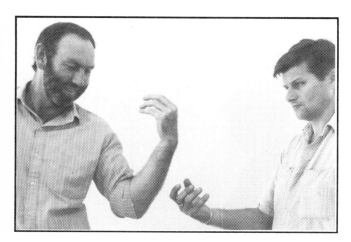

Picture 16. The worker bends the arm at the elbow for added strength and quickly twists up against the aggressor's thumb to gain release.

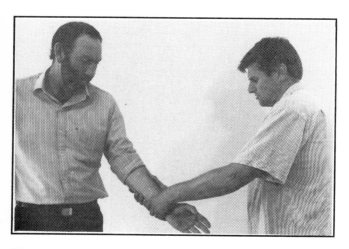

Picture 17.

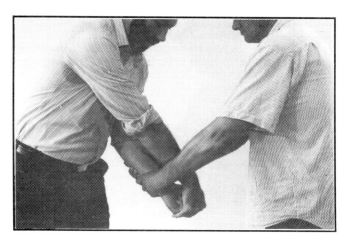

Picture 18.

Picture 19. The worker reaches in with their other hand, grasps the captured hand and pulls it free against the aggressor's thumb.

In attacks of punching, scratching or the grabbing of skin, hair or clothing, the best defence is also one which places the aggressor's hold in a position of mechanical disadvantage so that use of further force is difficult. The aim is to weaken the grip, not to cause pain nor lock the opponent's wrist joint.

Pictures 20 to 25 illustrate how in the case of hair grabbing the worker must first obtain control over the grabbing hand and then move it into a position of mechanical disadvantage.

When there is a need to release a firm grip on a body part or other object (eg a club), it is again necessary to firstly gain control over the grabbing hand. Then the thumb is moved into a position directly up against the knuckles. Without attempting to pull the thumb directly away from the rest of the hand, it is pushed towards the base of the index (first) finger. With the thumb removed, the strength of the grip is broken.

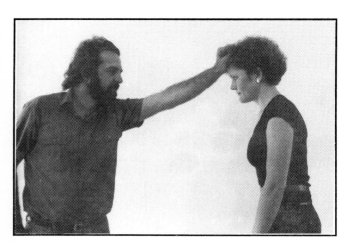

Picture 20.

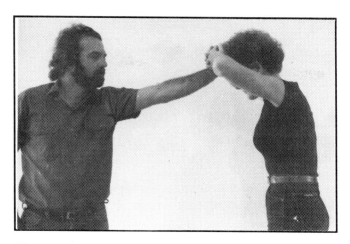

Picture 21.

Picture 22. The worker first gains control over the hand and then moves it into a mechanically disadvantaged position, while bringing the elbows down to protect the face and body.

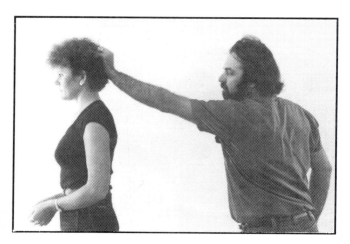

Picture 23

Picture 24

Picture 25. The worker gains control over the hand and moves the aggressor into a disadvantaged position by rapidly turning.

Defences Against Chokes

Although choking is a frightening experience, a worker will usually have several seconds to take action before losing consciousness.

The essential, primary response in such situations is for the worker to tuck their chin down as hard as possible against their chest. This protects vital air and blood vessels and makes it more difficult for an attacker to get a solid grip on the worker's neck.

In either a front or rear choke the worker drops their head, then raises one arm and turns, using twisting, torque and leverage to release the grip (pictures 26–31)

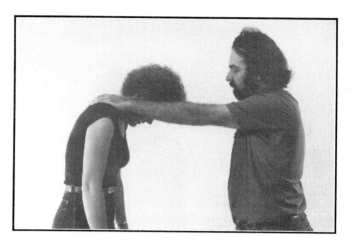

Picture 26.

Picture 27.

Picture 28. The worker first tucks in their chin and then raises one arm and turns it against the hands, breaking the choke.

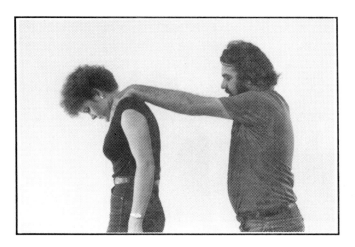

Picture 29.

Picture 30.

Picture 31. When choked from behind, the worker tucks in their chin, then raises one arm and turns it against the hands, breaking the choke.

In the case of an 'arm bar' choke, the first step is for the worker to tuck their chin behind the attacker's arm while using both hands to pull the attacker's arm down and away from the throat (picture 32). When the pressure is off the throat, the worker may decide to wait, negotiate, call for help or try to gain full release from the headlock by now pushing against the attacker's elbow and backing out (pictures 33, 34).

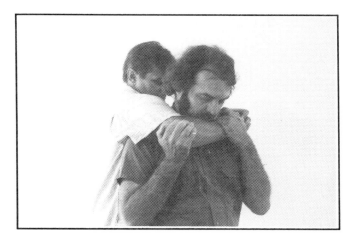

Picture 32.

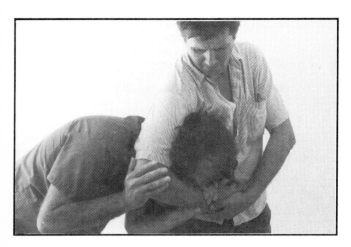

Picture 33.

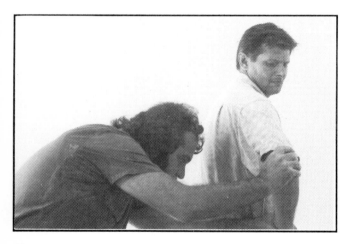

Picture 34. In an arm bar choke the worker tucks their chin in behind the aggressor's arm while pulling downwards and if possible backs out of the headlock.

Defence Against Bear Hugs

Holds of this type, though frightening, are not generally life threatening. Often the best response may be simply for the worker to lift their legs off the ground, letting the aggressor carry the worker's full weight and wait for them to tire.

The worker can then gradually prise themselves free by clasping their hands and pulling them upwards, while pushing outwards with their elbows. This adds pressure to the opponent's grip, forcing it further apart, while the worker turns their head to one side and slides down and through, moving quickly to the side, avoiding the possibility of a blow from the assailants knee (pictures 35–37).

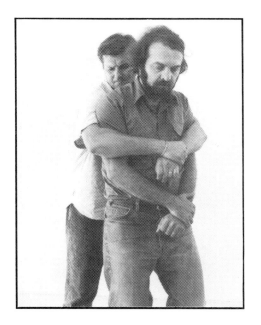

Picture 35.

Picture 36.

Picture 37 The worker lifts their legs slightly off the ground, turns their head to the side, pushes up with their arms and drops through.

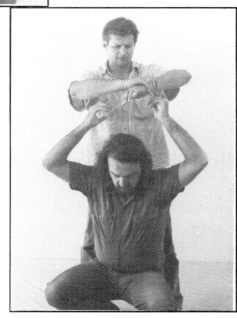

It is necessary to stress again, at this point, that all the above responses must be thoroughly practised and carefully implemented. Their use, however, cannot guarantee freedom from trauma due to violence, but may lessen, or avoid the harmful effects of such confrontations.

Here the basic principles outlined in this and previous chapters need to be placed in an overall frame work for managing aggression. This framework, the 'SACRED' approach is outlined in the next chapter.

Chapter Five. The 'SACRED' Approach To Managing Aggression

Putting It All Together.

A balanced approach to aggression management contains six major components. These components are usually run in sequence, though some parts may run in parallel, and others may be repeated in a cycle. These components are:

Self control
Analysis of the situation and the environment
Choice of strategies
Responding appropriately
Evaluation of effectiveness of interventions
Decision on next step

Each incident is a mini-drama with a beginning, middle and end, with countless structural variations, partly the result of the way the worker is directing the 'scene'. When dealing with the public, workers need to be masters of verbal persuasion. They must, as Thompson outlines, know their own perspective, know how to couch their communication, be sure of their purpose and be adept in structuring their message. They must be able to speak in many different ways to a variety of people.

Self Control in Human Service Workers

As previously mentioned, one area of great importance in dealing with violence is the worker's own self-understanding and control. Any violent situation is usually an interaction of a number of factors including the workers with their own world views, needs, fears, prejudices and past history.

Competent workers need to examine their own emotional and intellectual functioning in order to identify potential danger areas that can influence adversely their responses in conflict situations. Their past history and current world view can, when tested by a particular situation or difficult person, cause an over-reaction or inappropriate response of one type or another.

This is not saying that workers should deny or repress their feelings, but that they should acknowledge them and use them constructively.

Some typical staff responses to impending or actual situations of violence include:

- Denial: *'Nothing will happen'*;

- Helplessness: *'There is nothing I can do'*;

- Power fantasy: *'I can talk anyone down'*;

- Suppression: *'Let's not talk about such unpleasant possibilities'*;

- Repression: *'I don't feel anxious about possibly being attacked'*;

- Overreaction: *'People like him should be locked up'*.

Other responses may include denial of the person's access to a service or its benefits, inappropriate referral, decreased contact or increased control through medication.

Such coping strategies may be temporarily useful for the worker, but may soon prove destructive when carried on into any attempt at a helping relationship.

Most workers in a situation of conflict and violence will feel a sense of unease, apprehension and fear. Denying this will not help, but acknowledging it is the first step towards controlling it.

The other effect of the worker's particular bias and world view is that these may hamper the worker's ability to observe and understand the client's needs, feelings and reactions. The worker may not necessarily be overwhelmed emotionally in the situation, but may have certain perceptual or cultural blind spots that may lead to their misperceiving the situation and responding inappropriately.

Workers are to be encouraged to examine their emotional and intellectual make-up and to identify potential danger areas or weaknesses that can show in their responses. All workers need to examine their personal assumptions about the world—their world view. These gut level assumptions and responses are one of the greatest blocks to effective communication and skilful negotiation.

Workers, then, must analyse their past and their most strongly held assumptions and learn to integrate what they have been, and where they are, with who they must become, if they want to be effective in their work.

Workers wanting to control a communication situation must firstly learn to control themselves inwardly and outwardly and this begins with an awareness of SELF. Workers must learn to subsume their ego and sense of self into the many roles they must play. They need to improvise, given the differences of each 'scene', use the energies of their antagonists and react from a kind of 'still centre', as in the martial arts.

Analysing the Situation

In this next step the worker must learn to read the situation without bias or assumptions, in a state of assumed objectivity. Objectivity means free from bias, impartial; it doesn't mean uninterested or mechanical. It is seeing before judging, a state of mind that is as open and flexible as possible, ready to analyse the available cues and form appropriate responses to handle the situation.

The situation is made up of two variables: the participants involved and the environment or context.

Understanding the Participants

In order to understand those involved and the reasons for their actions, six crucial questions need to be asked at the scene:

- What has happened?

- Who is involved?

- Where did it occur?

- When did it occur?

- Why did it occur?

- How did it occur?

Attempting to answer these questions first, rather than deal with one's own pre-occupation or emotional state, helps delay judgments as long as possible.

Answering the WHY (causes) question is often crucial in deciding what strategy may best fit the situation. To look for causes before responding may prevent the mistaking of an accidental act for an intentional one.

Also, showing a person that the causes of their action are understood, though not necessarily condoned, may lessen their initial hostility towards the worker and improve the worker's chance of influencing the subject through words, not force.

During the initial stages of the worker's contact with an aggressive person a number of quick assessments need to be made in light of the what, who, where, when, why and how questions.

Many of these judgments need to be made in a split second, others may be made more slowly, and both have to be open to modification. These judgments form much of the basis for choosing intervention strategies. The worker needs to be able to make the following assessments of those involved:

What is the person's name?

What is their appearance? Age, sex, ethnic background, physical size and clothing style.

What is the worker's relationship with the person?

What sort of image is the person trying to present?

What are the aggressor's main objectives?

What are that person's stated and real needs?

What are their attitudes and prejudices?

What are the person's obvious strengths and weaknesses?

What power does the other person have?

What are the current emotional and psychological stressors in their life, such as loss or grief, disappointment, failure or frustration?

The worker may not be able to gather all this information but needs to be alert to what cues the aggressor is giving.

With the worker's entry into a situation, the scene automatically changes and the worker must be sensitive as to how the particpants saw the scene prior to their entry.

A worker may be able to understand the other's viewpoints and feelings by using techniques of suspension, projection and identification. This involves:

Initially suspending judgment and avoiding hasty reactions while analysing a dangerous or escalating situation;

Projecting themselves into the other's present situation in order to understand the other person and their current motives;

Identifying what they have, or can have, in common with the other, through:

• Finding parallels in the worker's own life experiences to the basic feelings and emotions shown by the other;

• Recalling a similar incident in the worker's own life and reliving the feelings and responses caused by it. This is called the 'spots of time' technique;

- Identifying the role the subject is playing, for example, cheated husband or macho man.

As the worker accurately assesses how subjects see themselves, their world view and the roles they play, they will have a better idea of what actions and words could escalate or defuse violent situations

Total situation awareness is the mental process of seeing fully the dynamics of the situation being faced. This leads the worker to be able to anticipate what could happen and make the necessary physical and verbal adjustments and approaches to deal with the situation.

Analysing the Environment

As with understanding those involved, there are a number of assessments about the environment that the worker must quickly undertake in order to make the best intervention choices. Such assessments are made on the basis of the answers to these questions:

- Is there anything that is reinforcing others' negative behaviour or might do so?

- Is there anything frightening the person?

- Is the environment over or understimulating?

Some factors that could reinforce negative behaviour or frighten a person could include:

- Changes of medication;

- Changes in living conditions;

- Entry or exit from an institution or program;

- Major changes in routine;

- Presence of additional staff or other people;

- Onset or recurrence of mental illness.

Some environmental factors that might influence a person's behaviour are:

- Space: too much, too little, no privacy;

- Light and colour: overstimulating or sterile;

- Noise, temperature, time of day, month or season.

In the light of the above analysis, certain intervention strategies may now seem the most appropriate.

Choosing Intervention Strategies

Ways of Determining Means and Ends

Determining the means is often a problem, as there may be several possible ways of successfully resolving a situation.

Deciding what option to take under particular constraints and problems can be helped by asking four questions about any possible means:

- **Practicality**: can the option be put into effect?

- **Economy**: is the option efficient and manageable?

- **Effectiveness**: does the option produce the desired effect?

- **Consistency**: is it consistent with present legal, ethical, social and personal values? Are these means consistent with the stated values of the end?

In any confrontational situation, workers have at least three sets of guidelines for responses to ensure that they will not react purely on gut level assumptions or the state of their emotions. The first two have already been mentioned:

- The six questions—what, who, where, when, why and how—in order to gather information;

- The four criteria—practicality, economy, effectiveness and consistency—that enable workers to consider options and select the most appropriate for the particular situation.

The third includes:

- The law, regulations or job demands. Here the worker must be familiar with their specific legal rights and responsibilities in situations of potential or actual violence.

Finally, in coming to a conclusion about which strategies are the most appropriate to defuse the violence, the worker needs to ask the following questions:

Why do I need or want to intervene ?	(Reason)
What do I specifically want to achieve?	(Outcome)
Which method should I use?	(Method)
What level of intervention is best?	(Level)
When do I intervene?	(Timing)

These questions can be expanded in more detail as follows:

Reasons for Intervention

These, in summary, are usually of two major, often interrelated, kinds:

- To inform or clarify a situation;

- To persuade, change ideas or influence behaviour.

Desired Outcomes

Generally it is desired that the situation would be resolved in a manner that is mutually acceptable to all the parties involved, that is, a win–win situation whenever possible.

Methods of Intervention

Verbal methods of persuasion can be used by themselves or in conjunction with other non-verbal strategies. The response options to actual or threatened violence are usually one or more of the following, as suggested by Dobson and Shepherd-Chow (1981):

- Negotiation

- Leaving (flight)

- No action

- Surprise or Diversion

- Blending

- Fighting

- Evasive self-defence

Level of Intervention

This involves the use of an appropriate balance of verbal and non-verbal techniques suitable to the person's current emotional and physical state.

Timing of Interventions

In dealing with stressed and aggressive people, the worker has to decide what is the best way to structure and when to present their communication, in order to achieve the desired resolution.

It is, again, important to note that the situation changes with the worker's entry into it and should develop in the light of how the worker handles it. Each scene has three major phases:

- **Opening Phase**

Any encounter has a beginning, middle and end. The opening phase is vital for the worker, for if it is mishandled there may be little possibility of success.

Here the worker's role is to analyse what is happening and establish their authority and control over the situation in a low-key, neutral and objective fashion.

- **Middle Phase**

Moving into this phase involves the adoption by the worker of the most appropriate role and strategies that the situation demands. This middle phase is largely a matter of trial and correction as strategies break down or new situations arise.

A major mistake to be avoided here is to back a person into a corner, leaving them with no way to escape or to maintain dignity and face. Many violent attacks occur from situations where people feel trapped and see no alternative but violent resistance.

- **Ending Phase**

The successful conclusion of an encounter involves the worker fulfilling their purpose and leaving those involved as well disposed towards the worker as is reasonably possible, creating a respect for what they have done. It is not always possible to please everyone, but even unpopular decisions can be made to be seen as unavoidable or morally and legally correct.

How a situation ends may be dependent on whether this is a once only or a continuing encounter. Also, the worker must be aware of how the other person sees the ending phase. A successful resolution for a worker may not be seen as such by the other person, or a soon forgotten encounter for the worker may continue to trouble the other involved.

Responding Appropriately

This involves the worker adopting a specific role for that particular audience and context. Such a role is not insincere, but is rather the adoption of a flexible way of dealing with a changing situation. The source of the aggression—from fear, frustration, manipulation, intimidation, pain or impairment—will help determine the appropriate intervention.

Aggression based on fear needs a response that attempts to remove any external threat to the aggressor while providing them with personal support. Responses to 'frustrated' violence need to be based on building alliances between the worker and the aggressor as well as encouraging the other's internal control. Attempts at manipulative violence need to be met with worker detachment and limit setting. Intimidatory violence may be best dealt with, in some situations, by pointing out the consequences of such acts for the aggressor. In extreme situations of intimidation the worker may seriously need to consider temporarily yielding to such demands for their own ultimate safety. Smith outlines in some detail what should be the worker's specific verbal and non-verbal responses to violent situations depending on its perceived source, be it fear, anger, manipulation or intimidation. These responses are as follows.

Threat Reduction

This involves the use of communication patterns that reduce the perceived threat. Posture is relaxed, with hands open and palms upward, gestures are slow, deliberate and reassuring. Position is slightly off to one side, at or below the other's eye level, not crowding the other. Voice usage is reassuring, encouraging and confident, promising to help if possible. Eye contact is used, if needed, for reassurance but not forced on the other. Physical contact may also be used, where applicable to indicate worker support.

Frustration Reduction

Here communication is used that demonstrates control and the ability to deal with the frustration. Posture is authoritative, gestures are strong and deliberate. The position taken is directly in front of the person, just outside of their striking range. Voice usage is commanding and firm in low tones, repetitive and confident, without threatening the other. Eye contact is direct, accompanied by facial expressions giving a sense of control. Physical contact, where necessary, should be firm without excessive movement and not inflicting pain or discomfort.

Manipulation Reduction

Communication patterns here are used to indicate a refusal to be involved in attempts at manipulation. The posture used is closed and relaxed. Positioning is far enough away to show non-involvement, possibly slightly away to show disinterest. The voice used is detached and slightly bored, using quiet, repetitive commands to 'calm down'. The worker should avoid responding to the demands underlying the manipulation until the other person is seated and calmed down. Eye contact is usually to be avoided, again to show lack of interest. Any necessary physical contact is to be done in a detached, non-involved manner.

Intimidation Reduction

Here the consequences or costs of intimidation through assault must be clearly communicated to the aggressor. Worker posture is poised, ready to react, but not in an obviously defensive or fearful fashion, and gesture usage is limited. Position is one of the greatest defensive advantage, perhaps using a piece of furniture as a barrier. Voice usage is matter of fact, with little emotion and a non-threatening tone, using clear repeated statements of the consequences of aggressive acts. Eye contact is used sparingly for emphasis, and physical contact, where needed, is undertaken quickly in a matter of fact way.

In the light of these sources of aggressive behaviour and particular responses to them, previously mentioned methods of intervention can now be dealt with in more detail.

Negotiation

General verbal strategies have already been examined, but negotiation is a specific response to aggression that should be attempted first in most situations.

The importance of negotiation strategies has been shown by Dubin and others. His survey of assault against psychiatrists is one of the few which assessed the effectiveness of verbal versus physical intervention in attempts to defuse a violent incident. In this survey, positive talking, negotiation strategies led to property damage in only 3% of cases and no physical injury whereas physically aggressive coping strategies led to personal injury of the therapist in 33% of the cases and property damage in 10% of situations.

Once the other's world view, position and feeling are understood (the analysis stage), there are certain negotiation approaches that can be taken. They should be done in a calm, easy style, speaking as to a friend or equal, not expressing or showing fear, anger or contempt. It is an attempt to negotiate from a position of equality and uses some of the following approaches.

Negotiation Approaches

- Let the participants know their position is clearly understood. Gauge what will motivate their self-interest;

- Show the other person the areas in which their viewpoint is correct, rather than initially the areas in which they are wrong. Identify the similarities between you both, rather than the differences;

- State why you are there, your role and how you see the situation. Doing these steps first may make the subject more receptive, creating a sense of mutual understanding, 'I've listened to you, now hear my side';

- Demonstrate how others would benefit from accepting the worker's position. Show that all involved will benefit, rather than the worker stressing only their own interest. Redirect the aggressor's energies from harming others towards benefiting themselves.

Anything that workers can do to show themselves more understanding and human will usually increase their chances of succeeding without becoming victims of violence.

How to Negotiate

In any negotiations situation there are four possible outcomes in terms of final results:

I win – you lose
I lose – you win
I lose – you lose
I win – you win

The fourth possibility, in which both parties have gained something and maintained face is, obviously, the best. The win–win style needs to be deeply ingrained in the worker's approaches, becoming a habitual way of thinking and responding.

When to Negotiate

• Where the assailant gives signs of being open to approaches or wanting acceptance. Where possible don't grant acceptance until the assailant is willing to compromise or to take a more positive course of action;

• Where there may be points of similarity such as gender, age, ethnic background;

• When more time is needed, negotiation can keep the assailant talking or listening. If they won't listen to reason get them to talk about their own concerns and grievances, as long as this doesn't further inflame their feelings;

• Where an assailant needs help to back down from an aggressive stand they have taken, or is confused or uncertain of what next step to take.

Here the worker can tactfully sum up the situation for them as a no-win situation. Outline the options and suggest ways of making it a win-win situation.

When Not to Negotiate

- When there is no time and immediate action is called for;

- When the assailant is incapable of understanding the worker through handicap, language barrier or physical condition. Attempts to negotiate here may spark further hostility and frustration;

- When an aggressor is too mentally unbalanced, hostile or drugged to respond to reason;

The Leaving Option

Another option that a worker should not hesitate to use, if necessary, is that of leaving the situation, the strategy of flight.

When to Leave

- The moment a situation seems totally uncontrollable, leave quickly. Consider delaying only if an early escape increases risk of re-capture, or possible injury to others or the aggressor in the situation;

- When a crowd or group a worker is in suddenly gets agitated, leave as quickly and carefully as possible;

- Leave when assailants drop their guard, become distracted or make a mistake;

Before leaving, consider what must be done to escape and where is the nearest place of safety.

How to Leave

- Don't run as a panic reaction, but a positive action. Run towards a place of safety not just away from danger;

- Once started, don't hesitate or stop until free and clear;

- In a confined or cluttered environment, don't run at full speed and risk running into something. Keep the speed down until the field is clear. Put obstacles between yourself and your pursuers, do whatever is necessary to slow them down, tire or distract them;

- If it will help, take off shoes to make running easier and quieter;

- Consider while running: where to run to; how far is it; what is the best way there?

- Have an alternative plan if the original one doesn't work.

Who to Run From

- Assailants with an obvious physical advantage or fighting ability;

- A suicidal person or one who believes they have nothing to lose;

- Those who are under the influence of drugs or mentally unbalanced;

- Agitated people defending their own territory or personal space;

- Rapists or those intent on sexual abuse of a worker.

The No Action Option

This is a deliberate choice of action in order to achieve a later, more favourable, situation. Such a choice acknowledges control over yourself, if not, as yet, of the situation. No action can range from freezing to ignoring or continuing current actions. Freezing should be used as a conscious choice and not as a fear response.

When to Take No Action

- When there are no other options. Centre self, save energy and plan ahead;

- When uncertain, upset or caught off guard. Wait until the situation becomes clearer;

- If the situation seems to be improving;

- When confronted with weapons or by those on drugs or mentally unbalanced;

- When your actions might jeopardise others' lives (e.g. displace violence onto others). Don't act unless lives are in immediate, obvious danger.

When to Take Action

- When delay may cause further deterioration of the situation;

- When flight, negotiation or other options are viable;

- When early objection shows you do not condone particular acts of victimisation. Non-response may lead the assailant to feel encouraged in victimising others.

Surprise or Diversion Option

Surprise is a sudden change of mood, focus or direction. Diversion may include the above and distraction but at a slower pace and could involve suggesting other, non-violent activities such as offering refreshments.

Here the objective is to interrupt the attacker's train of thought or action, confusing them or re-focussing their attention on something else. This creates an opportunity for the worker to take control of the situation or to escape.

Workers need to be aware of the possible use of surprise/diversion as a way of changing a situation or as using an unexpected development that can work to their advantage.

Initiating Surprise/Diversion

- Make a sudden unexpected action: collapse; fake unconsciousness, a fit or a heart attack; freak out or feign insanity. All of these can be very disconcerting to an assailant;

- Use humour, when least expected, to defuse a situation;

- Scream or shout. This can be quite unnerving, especially after a period of silence;

- Bluff.

When to Surprise/Divert

- When an assailant is obviously insecure or confused and unsure of what to do;

- When there is some kind of external distraction taking the immediate focus off the worker;

- If the situation seems really hopeless and only some type of bizarre, unexpected behaviour may have an effect.

When Not to Surprise/Divert

- With an assailant who seems calm, alert and fully in control. Here attempts to stall or divert may make the situation worse;

- Where an assailant seems agitated, excited or paranoid or has a weapon;

- Where there are multiple assailants.

The Blending Option

Blending involves a temporary re-direction of a worker's energy to blend with, and reinforce the energies of the assailant rather than opposing them.

This unexpected blending of forces may surprise and unbalance the attacker, giving the worker an opportunity to take control or flee immediately.

Blending can be used effectively for both verbal and physical attacks. The type of blending to use will be defined by the situation.

How to Blend

*   Where possible empathise with the assailant, as the more the worker is able to relate to them, the more able they will be to anticipate their actions and move the assailants towards more acceptable options;

*   Relax completely, offer no resistance;

*   Suddenly join your force with theirs, moving in the same direction as the attacker's energy, unbalancing them.

When to Blend

*   When there is no other choice;

*   When time is needed to decide what other options best suit the situation.

Blending is an active alternative to no action when more time to plan is needed or the time to act has not yet come.

The Fight Option

This should only happen as a last resort, when no other options seem available, in order to save a life or avoid major injury.

When to Fight

• When a violent unprovoked attack is made at close quarters with immediate danger of severe physical harm to a worker— assuming flight is not an option;

• When someone else's life is in danger and their safety is dependent on the worker's immediate and forceful intervention;

• When a situation is seriously deteriorating and fighting now will prevent the worker having to act from a less advantageous position.

When Not to Fight

• Where flight or other options are still available;

• When persuasion can still stop an attack;

• When the assailants have weapons that they will use;

• When help is coming and the assailant can be stalled or diverted.

Who Not to Fight

• A suicidal person or one who believes they have nothing to lose, such as cases of murder–suicides, and political or religious fanatics;

• Those under the influence of drugs or mentally unbalanced

• Someone threatening violence against a person in your care;

• Agitated people defending their own territory or personal space.

Evasive Self-Defence

This was covered already in the previous chapter and, as previously noted, it is only used in order to enable a worker to avoid personal injury or to escape from a dangerous situation. It should be used with negotiation whenever possible.

After using any of the above responses, the worker then needs to assess their effectiveness.

Evaluating Intervention Outcomes

This involves the worker in assessing their own performance in intervening in the situation in the light of the SACRED response strategy.

S   Was the worker self aware and in control of their situation?
A   Did they analyse the situation correctly?
C   Was the best intervention strategy chosen?
R   Did the worker respond appropriately?

Deciding Future Actions

In the light of such ongoing evaluation the worker should make decisions about what their next action will be. Future action could include stopping, modifying or continuing the current intervention.

However, even the most skilled worker may not be able to totally control or prevent acts of violence or aggression against others or themselves. The question of post-trauma support for Human Service Workers who have become victims of violence, needs to be more widely examined in the light of worker's responses to being both helper and victim. These issues will be considered in the next chapter.

Chapter Six. The Hurting Helper

The Effects of Violence on Human Service Workers

There has been increasing research in recent years on the effects of criminal and violent behaviour on victims. The investigation of the psychological responses to violent assault has noted that the reactions of victims of such assaults parallel the reactions of individuals to other traumatic environmental stressors (Kahn, 1984).

Before proceeding to discuss the limited literature on the reactions of Human Service Workers to assaultive behaviour, it is useful to note some key issues from the much more developed research in the general population, with respect to individuals' responses, not only to violence and assaultive behaviour, but also to other traumatic environmental stressors.

Human Responses to Trauma

In recent years the reactions of individuals to traumatic environmental stressors has received considerable attention. The occurrence of long term stress reactions to catastrophic environmental events has long been documented in the medical and psychiatric literature (Lifton, 1983), and the phenomenon that is now most frequently termed Post Traumatic Stress Disorder (PTSD) has previously been given a variety of labels, including traumatic hysteria, traumatic neurosis and situational crisis. However, in 1980, PTSD formed a new diagnostic category in the Diagnostic and Statistical Manual of the American Psychiatric Association (DSM III) (APA, 1980), and explicit diagnostic criteria were specified. According to DSM III, PTSD is a psychological reaction to those traumatic events that are generally regarded as being beyond the normal or common range of human experience. Much research has focused on reactions to such environmental stressors as man made and natural disasters.

The symptoms of PTSD have also been noted, however, after solitary catastrophes such as rape, violent assault, motor vehicle crashes and industrial accidents (Kaplan and Saddock, 1981).

Here it should be noted that the DSM III has been recently revised and this revision has been the source of heated debate about whether this new classification was needed or is useful. As much of the research referred to in this book occurred before this revision, and because of the ongoing debate about its usefulness, the DSM III classification is used here.

DSM III includes the following general criteria to describe a post traumatic stress disorder:

- The existence of a recognisable external stressor;

- Recurrent and intrusive waking recollections or dreams of the traumatic event or suddenly acting as if the event were occurring again in response to some triggering stimulus;

- A numbed responsiveness to the external world;

Plus the appearance of at least two of the following symptoms absent before the trauma:

- Exaggerated startle response;

- Sleep disturbance;

- Guilt;

- Memory impairment or trouble concentrating;

- Phobic reactions;

- Intensification of symptoms when exposed to situations that resemble the traumatic event.

Post-traumatic reactions tend to vary greatly in intensity and duration and are influenced by a number of situational and personality variables. Symptoms of the disorder may be experienced immediately, or may have a delayed onset varying from a few hours to some years. DSM III criteria suggest that if symptoms occur within six months of the trauma or the duration is less than six months, the disorder is considered acute. Chronic PTSD is defined as a syndrome appearing later than six months or a syndrome with symptoms that last for more than six months, and, while this is less common, it is more handicapping.

According to Kaplan and Saddock, most cases of PTSD are acute, in that symptoms do not typically persist for longer than six months, and in many such cases the symptoms resolve without specific intervention.

Post traumatic stress reactions have been observed in numerous individuals across a large variety of situations. Nevertheless, it has been noted that both situational and personality variables influence individuals' reactions to traumatic environmental events. Situational variables that have been found to influence an individual's response to traumatic events have included: extent of life threat; degree of bereavement; speed of onset and duration of the trauma; potential for reoccurrence of the trauma; and the degree of exposure to death, dying and destruction (Wilson, Smith and Johnson, 1985).

Kaplan and Saddock also note that, in addition to the presence of, or the ability to develop, adequate coping mechanisms, two other broad categories of personality variables also influence post trauma stress reactions. These are the presence of any pre-existing psychiatric or psychological difficulties and the availability of social supports. The impact of particular stressors tends to be increased for those individuals with pre-existing difficulties and for those with impoverished or absent social support networks.

Assault and Violence as Traumatic Stressors

The American Psychological Association convened a special Task Force on the Victims of Crime and Violence (Kahn, 1984). to review, among other issues, the state of psychological knowledge on victimisation and to survey theory and approaches to interventions for helping those who have been victimised.

The task force noted that the experience of being victimised has profound psychological consequences, both immediate and long term, and the 'personal disruption of feelings and behaviour can range from relatively short term discomfort to a disabling long term post traumatic stress disorder' (Kahn, p. 24).

Much research with victims of both violent and assaultive behaviour, as well as research with victims of other traumatic environmental stressors, has noted surprising commonality in individuals' responses, with their reactions following a predictable sequence. There has been a number of attempts to categorise the reactions into stages (e.g. Bard and Sangrey, 1979; Mitchell & Resnik, 1981, National Organizations for Victim Assistance, NOVA, undated), some of which are outlined below.

Immediate Reactions

The immediate reaction has been labeled the 'impact disorganisation phase' by Bard and Sangrey. They suggest it is characterised by numbness or disorientation, denial, disbelief, and feelings of loneliness, depression, vulnerability and helplessness. Alternatively, Mitchell and Resnik suggest that this phase may be characterised by hyperactivity. Another type of initial reaction or perhaps a second phase of this immediate reaction stage, termed 'frozen fright', may also occur, in which the victim feels a pseudo-calm detachment that may last from hours to days (Symonds 1976). Frederick (1980) suggests that anxiety and sleep disturbances are the most common immediate reactions to violence. However, a variety of other physiological reactions may occur, including headaches, an increase in psychosomatic symptoms and an aggravation of previous medical problems. Frederick further notes that these immediate physical reactions rapidly diminish, but 'if treatment is not instituted or supports are hostile or unavailable, they can become long-term' (Kahn, p. 25).

Short-term Reactions

With regard to short term reactions, Bard and Sangrey have termed the next stage 'recoil', lasting from three to eight months, they suggest that victims in this stage may experience emotional reactions which swing from fear to anger, sadness to elation and self pity to guilt.

Victims in this stage may also experience a loss of identity and self respect, and often feel rejection by others and an erosion of trust and autonomy. Many of the behavioural reactions symptomatic of post traumatic stress disorder also appear, including insomnia, restlessness, uncontrollable crying, agitation, increased drug use, and intrusive and persistent thoughts about the traumatic event when both awake and asleep. Fear and avoidance behaviour are also indicative of post traumatic stress reactions. Krupnick and Horowitz (1981) suggest that one of the most prominent themes expressed by personal injury and assault victims is fear of repetition of the event and feelings of responsibility for it occurring.

As mentioned above, there is generally a decrease of symptoms within six months of a traumatic event. However a variety of factors may influence the course of individual's reactions. Kahn notes that, whether or not a victim develops post-traumatic stress disorder depends, in part, on their psychological strength prior to the trauma, the nature of the trauma and how severely the incident violates the individual's self integrity.

Kahn further notes that individuals' strong and often conflicting reactions during the second stage, suggest that they are especially responsive to social support during that period. Depending on their coping skills and social supports, the personal reorganisation that occurs may be either adaptive or maladaptive.

Longer Term Reactions

The final reaction stage ideally involves some reorganisation. Symonds states that victims may resolve the trauma of victimisation by developing more effective defensive and vigilant behaviours, and revising their values and attitudes. However as Kahn indicates, long term reactions can continue to be problematic. Research with rape victims has in fact noted that individuals may report more symptoms twelve months later than they did three and six months after the event.

Explaining Reactions to Assault and Violence

A variety of factors have been suggested by different writers to explain an individual's reactions to assault and violence. Whilst there is agreement that being victimised is an inherently stressful experience, differing explanations are offered as to the precise source of the stress. General stress theories have been applied to victimisation, and it has been noted that victims' responses to victimisation parallel the reaction of individuals to other, traumatic, environmental stressors. Within this framework, issues such as expectations about, and appraisal of, the traumatic event, life history of prior stressors, personal characteristics such as fears and self confidence, and social status, may all influence an individual's reaction.

Other researchers have focused on the experience of victimisation and suggest that other critical issues in influencing an individual's reactions relate to a sense of violation of the self, feeling of inequity, vulnerability to additional victimisation and the perception of oneself as deviant.

Coping with Assaults and Violence

For victims, a crisis may be accompanied by a number of losses and destruction of cherished beliefs. These can include:

- Loss of control of one's life, present and future;

- Loss of trust in God or other people;

- Loss of a sense of a just and fair world;

- Loss of a self image of being worthwhile;

- Loss of a sense of invulnerability and immortality.

Janoff-Bulman (1983) suggests that there are two main types of coping strategies used by victims to cope with these losses:

- Intrapsychic/cognitive responses;

- Direct action or behavioural responses.

Intrapsychic Responses

Such responses are the emotional and psychological reactions to trauma and may include:

Redefining the event

Rationalisations may be used that involve comparing the self with others who were much worse off as victims, or by trying to perceive some lesson, experience or benefit that might be gained from the event. Additionally, attempts may be made to explain away or reappraise the severity of the event or to find some type of meaning or purpose behind it. If some sense of purpose can be found then victims can begin to re-establish a belief in an orderly, understandable world.

Self blame

Another common cognitive mechanism victims use in an attempt to reappraise an assault is self blame. In assigning blame for their victimisation, individuals may make a variety of attributions, that is, judgements about themselves. Attribution theory would make predictions about the emotional and behavioural consequences of such attributions. For example, blaming one's character as the reason for being victimised might lead to a sense of hopelessness about the future and would initially appear somewhat maladaptive. However, Kahn suggests that such self blame can be functional, especially if the victim blames their actions rather than their personality. Thus acceptance of behavioural responsibility is seen as providing an individual with 'agenda control' (Peterson and Seligman, 1983), that is, with a sense of control over the planning, choosing, and changing of the course of events in their life.

Kahn believes that behavioural blame can be a particularly effective intervention as it addresses the three major assumptions that have been shattered, namely: invulnerability, meaning and self esteem. The victim can, once again, believe in some control over, and protection from, events. They are also given some reason for the event occurring, why they behave that way, and an opportunity to build once again a positive self image.

However, such behavioural blame can prove to be quite maladaptive in the longterm if it reinforces or builds a delusional system or a false sense of control. Kahn's suggestion that such behaviour is in someway adaptive is seriously questioned by some authors and researchers such as Raphael.

Direct Action Responses

Direct action responses by victims can further rebuild the shattered assumptions of invulnerability, meaning and self esteem.

Direct action may provide a renewed sense of control over the immediate environment and serve to minimise this new sense of vulnerability, as well as helping re-establish a view of the world as being somewhat responsive to an individual's efforts. Such perceptions of control also help re-develop a positive self image and renew a sense of one's own abilities and autonomy.

Direct action can include reporting an offence, taking legal action, increasing security, lobbying for organisational change, moving location, taking self defence classes or further training.

It can also include seeking social support. Establishing or re-establishing support networks further enable victims to re-develop basic assumptions about their own self worth, while also seeing parts of the world, at least, as benevolent again. The failure to receive such support or have it given in an unacceptable fashion may lead to 'secondary injury'.

Thus, any successful resolution of a crisis situation involves dealing with loss, the related grief and bereavement and helping the person reconstruct their shattered beliefs and regain some control over their lives.

This rebuilding and recovery involves the following issues:

- Making sense of, or re-defining, the event;

- Re-establishing a sense of control over one's life;

- Restoring a feeling of trust and self worth;

- Re-establishing meaning and purpose and justice;

- Re-establishing balance and planning for the future.

The NOVA training program summarises these issues as the need to establish a climate of safety and security; ventilation and validation; prediction and preparation.

Effects of Victimisation on Significant Others

It has been noted that the 'illusion of invulnerability' protects most people from the stress and anxiety associated with the threat of assault or violence. This illusion, however, is seriously threatened when someone close to a member of a work, family or other personal or social group is victimised.

At a time when social support needs are critical, victims may find themselves socially isolated, not only because they might be depressed and unhappy individuals, but also because their presence is often an unwanted reminder to others of their own vulnerability.

Social support for victims might also be minimised because they are seen as losers. Assumptions regarding a just world (Lerner, 1980) are very powerful and such assumptions imply that victims are responsible for their fate and thus deserving of blame and derogatory comments rather than sympathy and support.

In the light of the above information, how do Human Service Workers react to being victims themselves?

Helping Professionals as Victims

There is little research on the impact of victimisation on Human Service Workers. Some of the available research tends to focus on the impact of disaster situations on individuals who are both victims and helpers during disaster situations. From the research on these groups we can gain information which may be useful in dealing with Human Service Workers as victims.

During Disasters

Raphael, Singh & Bradbury (1980) comment on two clear cut kinds of roles popularly associated with people affected by natural and man made disasters. These two roles are polarised into that of victims, 'who are seen as resourceless, weak, helpless', and, helpers 'who are seen as being resourceful, strong and powerful' (p. 445).

They focus on helpers involved in disaster situations such as disaster control and direct rescue personnel, medical and paramedical staff, information, communication and transport personnel as well as other support staff for the injured and their families. Amongst such workers are a variety of highly trained, untrained, full time, part time and voluntary workers.

It seems that rescuer victims, similar to the normal population, exhibit certain characteristics during and after a crisis situation, whether man made or natural. They also typically move through the emotional phases of reaction and resolution to a crisis event, as previously outlined.

Raphael et al further comment that disaster workers come to terms with the impact of the event on their lives in a whole variety of individual ways.

Some workers find that initially, traumatic memories, flashbacks and dreams about the event intrude into their working and sleeping time. For some, these intrusive events do not decrease over time and they are left with a chronic Post Traumatic Stress Disorder which slows long term recovery.

Helpers as Victims of Assault and Aggression

The little research and observational evidence available on the response of human service workers to assault and violence shows their reactions parallel those of non-helper victims. It is also noteworthy that the reaction of significant others, including their own helper colleagues, often contains the same negative and unhelpful elements as the reactions of non-helper workers to peers who are assaulted (Rowett 1986), the previously mentioned secondary injury.

Disaster workers and related Human Service Workers often face 'aggression' from natural or man made calamities, but not generally from the people they are trying to help. However, those Human Service Workers involved in more direct daily contact with troubled people are vulnerable to verbal or physical attacks by them. While with face to face helpers a crisis response may occur as the result of any traumatic stress, the stress caused by verbal and physical assault by those they are trying to help, may have some unique effects as outlined below.

Firstly, it is often sudden, arbitrary, unexpected and unpredictable. Its lack of predictability and its apparent randomness often gives the 'helper victim' no time to erect psychological and physical defences. They may be forced into a reactive, helpless coping pattern.

Secondly, an attack may cause the victim to lose a sense of control over their life and physical being, sometimes only for seconds but on occasions for hours. No longer do they feel in control of themselves.

Thirdly, though the attack may indeed have been arbitrary, the helper victim may feel chosen for the attack, and blame themselves for attracting the attacker. They find it difficult within their world view to accept their assault as a random event.

Fourthly, the professional training and socialisation of Human Service Workers emphasises being competent and in control and makes it extremely difficult and confusing for them when placed in a dependent, victim role. Mitchell (1984) expresses this well when commenting on rescue workers:

*They were trained only to be helpers, not victims. The neces-
sity to be both helper and victim generally produces a psychological conflict that makes people particularly vulnerable to
stress reactions, which are characterised by severe fatigue,
confusion, denial and withdrawal'* (p. 28).

Responses of Helpers to Victimisation

Like other victims, Human Service Workers have three types of
shared assumptions about themselves and the world shattered
by victimisation:

• The belief in their own invulnerability;

• Their perception of the world as a meaningful and com-
   prehensible place— a just world;

• That they are worthy decent people, due the respect of
   others, and having high self-esteem.

As with other victims, the Human Service Workers respond to
the shattering of these assumptions following assault with a
variety of emotional and physical responses. Anger, fear or
depression can emerge, making a return to work, or an ongoing
helpful attitude, difficult to maintain.

This was shown in Holden's survey which revealed a wide
variety of responses to aggression by the Victorian nurses.
61.9% felt angry, 41% anxious, 34.5% helpless, 30.6% afraid,
and 30% resentful. Among the various categories of staff sampled, student nurses reported the highest levels of anxiety
(66%); registered nurses the most resentment (33%); and charge
nurses the highest levels of anger (73.4%) and helplessness
(45%).

Dubins' survey of assaulted psychiatrists showed a variety of
emotional responses to the events. 30% were afraid of being
hurt, 22% were afraid of being killed, 14% felt angry, 11% con-
centrated on remaining calm and 10% had a desire to help the
patient.

Because of such feelings, workers may insist on the discharge, referral or breaking of contact with a violent patient or client. If assaulted staff feel that outward expression of their anger or fear is not allowed or is inappropriate, they may find indirect methods of expressing their feelings or of re-directing them elsewhere, perhaps against the other person, themselves, their family or staff. These feelings may also be directed against the organisation and its management and safety procedures.

Often, if the outward expression of these emotions is blocked, a sense of frustration, powerlessness and depression may increase. Lenehan and Turner (1984) have noted that symptoms of clinical depression among Human Service Workers after a violent incident are common. Symptoms noted have included: sadness and crying spells, feeling of worthlessness and emptiness, lack of direction and motivation, fatigue and irritability, sleep and eating disturbances.

Responses of Helpers' Significant Others

As alluded to previously, significant others in the life of the assaulted staff member may fend off insecurities about their own possible vulnerability by blaming the assaulted staff member for what has befallen them.

Blaming the helper-victim assists other staff members to distance themselves from the possibility of their also being violated too. Thus the helper-victim may be labeled by others as unprofessional, aggressive, careless, or angry. It would seem that the more traumatic or embarrassing the assault, the more others will continue the victimisation through secondary injury or trauma. This may be as devastating to the helper victim as the original trauma.

Such blaming and distancing behaviour has been well illustrated by Rowett in his survey of assault against social workers in England. Of the 450 replies to his questionnaire, 112 Social Workers (25%) reported that they had been assaulted, while a quarter of these assessed their injuries as moderate to severe.

The 30 assaulted Field Social Workers were matched for sex, age, work experience, shift structure and work place with 30 non-assaulted Field Social Workers. A similar matching exercise was conducted for 30 assaulted Residential Care Social Workers with 30 non-assaulted Residential Care Social Workers.

In subsequent interviews with the sample of 120 Social Workers it emerged that both assaulted and non-assaulted workers stereotyped assaulted workers as being more provocative, incompetent, authoritarian, and inexperienced. They characterised assaulted workers as those who:

- sought out riskier situations;

- challenged and confronted clients unnecessarily;

- were more demanding and less flexible;

- were less able to detect potentially violent situations, or to handle them once they occurred.

However when assaulted workers were asked to reflect upon their own responses and involvement in violent situations, the picture presented was quite different. 40% of the incidents were claimed to be totally the client's fault, while 60% of incidents were said to be due to faulty interaction between worker and client.

While Rowett's research shows no difference in characteristics, attitudes or approaches of the assaulted workers compared to the non-assaulted workers, the label of ineptitude or personal defect in the handling of violent situations was strongly used and maintained against those who had been assaulted.

Rowett asks the question as to why assaulted social workers, while recognising that they do not fit their own negative image of assaulted social workers, continue to hold the same stereotype of assaulted social workers as a group.

He suggests that perhaps they did not wish to see their own incident of assault as being a test of the stereotype that assaulted social workers are more aggressive, incompetent, etc. He also attempts to explain the gross under-reporting of assault by workers as a way of preventing others from testing out this stereotype against them as well.

Even where workers want to be supportive to a victimised colleague there are certain problems that must be faced and overcome.

Levy and Brown (1984) note five possible major barriers to a helper's ability to deal with a victim. These five barriers may also be present between staff victim and colleague helper. The five barriers are:

- Lack of objectivity;

- Lack of skills;

- Lack of understanding;

- Lack of confidence;

- Environmental barriers.

The helper experiencing a lack of objectivity may find that their feelings about the helper-victim interfere with appropriate responses. A helper lacking skills may not be able to deal with the issues involved or understand their fellow worker's particular needs and feelings. This, in turn, may lead to a lack of confidence in their ability to be supportive to an assaulted worker. Added to these barriers may be environmental barriers such as agency policy, procedures or lack of resources.

In the light of all the above factors, it is not surprising that one common response by assaulted workers to this process of victimisation is that of depression. This major problem for Human Service Workers is examined in the next chapter.

Chapter Seven. The Valley of Shadows

Depression In Human Service Workers

This chapter will look at one particular response by Human Service Workers to being the object of violence by others: the response of depression. Perhaps, to some, such a chapter in a book on dealing with violence may seem inappropriate. However, in the author's experience, the response of depression by assaulted workers is a common, but often misunderstood, problem that needs to be addressed.

Depression is no respecter of persons and may affect both the client/patient and the apparently more competent and caring professional in a deep way.

Flach (1986, p. 38) describes the type of person who may be susceptible to depression as one who is conscientious, responsible and as having a high personal ethic. They are a person who cares about the feelings of others and has a strong need to be liked and respected and is vulnerable to anything that would reduce their worth in the eyes of others or themselves. Such a person often has difficulty setting limits, is long suffering in the extreme and may carry a lot of suppressed and unrecognised anger.

Many of the above characteristics are the ones prized and encouraged in human service workers as being part of their training and role.

Types Of Depression

Depression can present itself in a variety of forms, showing different expressions from person to person, while having a marked effect upon a person's mood, thinking, behaviour and physical state.

As depression can occur in different forms there are also a number of apparent causes, and sometimes no obvious cause. This in turn can lead to a number of different ways of treating depression depending upon its type.

Modern research suggests that there are several types of depressive illnesses, or affective disorders, to give them the more correct title. Over recent years there has been a lot of debate as to how affective illnesses should be classified in terms of subcategories. P. Mitchell (1988) summarises the key questions in the debate as follows. 'Are there 2 distinct forms of depression, i.e. the endogenous ('psychotic') and reactive ('neurotic') forms, or do these represent the extremes of a single continuum of depression?' (p.13)

However, there is general agreement as to what constitute the core symptoms of depression. The Diagnostic and Statistical Manual (DSM III) lists these key symptoms as including depressed mood plus at least four of the following:

- Changed eating habits, appetite loss or gain, increased weight or loss of weight;

- Disturbed sleeping patterns, insomnia or over-sleeping, hypersomnia;

- Increased or decreased physical activity, agitation or retardation, not merely the subjective emotional feelings of the above;

- Loss of interest or pleasure in usual activities including decreased sexual drive;

- Loss of energy, chronic fatigue;

- Excessive feelings of worthlessness, self condemnation or inappropriate guilt;

- Increased inability to concentrate or make decisions, slowed thinking;

- Recurrent feelings of hopelessness, thoughts of dying or suicide attempts.

Some of these symptoms are found in all forms of depression, with each type displaying a unique syndrome of symptoms.

This chapter will deal mainly with reactive rather than endogenous depression. Reactive depression, as the name implies, comes about as a response to the pressures faced by workers in their work and personal lives. Endogenous depression has a number of features that seem to separate it from the reactive type, its lack of a readily identifiable 'cause' or triggering event being a key feature. Workers may be vulnerable to either type of depression and need to make themselves familiar with the symptoms and the treatment approaches used in both situations. (See Flach 1986, Bowie 1988a or P. Mitchell 1988).

Masked Depression

From the above list of signs of depression it is obvious that depression does not only show itself as despair, sadness or lowered affect. It also can appear in a disguised or 'masked' form, making it often difficult to diagnose or for a sufferer to recognise its presence. *Depression wears many masks. It may come disguised by phobias, obsessions, compulsions or the need to consult a gynaecologist. It may be mistaken for three-day baby blues or be coloured by psychotic delusions. It may wear the mask of senility or confusion.* (White, 1982, p. 92)

Such masked depression may continue to be unrecognised, its effects unheeded and its correct treatment neglected. Hart (1984) outlines some of the more general signs of masked depression as follows:

- Outbursts of anger;

- Compulsive work habits;

- Ineffectiveness at work, including boredom and interpersonal conflicts;

- Sense of loss of ambition, purpose or calling in life;

- Changed habits;

- Loss of sexual drive;

- Physical symptoms.

However, Hart cautions against automatically assuming that someone showing some of the above signs has masked depression. There is, of course, the opposite danger that an underlying masked depression may stay unrecognised or be treated inappropriately.

While it is not safe to assume that anyone displaying some of these symptoms has masked depression, such signs should not be ignored or superficially treated. For example, treatment for eating disorders, phobias, impotency or work related stress may not prove helpful if an underlying depression remains untreated.

Depression, Stress And Burnout

One further area worthy of investigation is the inter-relationship between depression, stress and burnout. The availability of additional information about such interactions may prove a useful preventative function in alerting Human Service Workers to potential depression 'causing' situations.

Studies on the relationship between depression and stress have not been conclusive and have generated three main viewpoints:

- There is no direct association between stress and primary depressive illness;

- Depression can produce stress in individuals predisposed to affective disorders. People with such tendencies can display abnormal reactions to normal stress situations;

- Stress can play a role in bringing on the affective disorder, especially in individuals who are genetically or developmentally predisposed to such disorders.

Uncertainty also exists about the relationship between depression and professional burnout.

Firth et al (1986) have described burnout as 'a complex of psychological responses (strain) to the very particular stress of constant interaction with other people in need' (p. 633). They note that much of the discussion to date on burnout lacks a coherent theoretical base and has been largely descriptive in nature.

However, despite this lack of theoretical coherency, Freudenberger and Richardson (1985) attempt to outline some connection between particular types of depression and burnout. They seek to differentiate between depression related to burnout and depression not related to burnout through two main criteria:

- Non-burnout related depression they see as being long term and affecting all areas of the sufferer's life, whereas burnout associated depression is usually short term in nature and specifically related to one area of the person's life;

- In non-burnout related depression, they suggest that the sufferer is likely to feel a sense of profound guilt over all that is seeming to go wrong in their life while the burnout related depressive is most likely to feel anger.

The burnout syndrome has been described as including symptoms such as guilt, pessimism, apathy, depression and decreased self esteem as well as physical/emotional exhaustion, psychosomatic illness, sleep difficulties and drug abuse. Negative attitudes to those being helped and to work, as well as absenteeism, are also seen as burnout symptoms.

However, a recent summary of the current burnout research makes the following comments about the above supposed symptoms of burnout: 'Research does not yet support inclusion of (these) symptoms and components authors speak to in ... burnout's definition. They may be correlates of, but do not seem to comprise, its prime dimension' (Perlman & Hartman 1982). They further suggest that future burnout research would 'benefit from a focus on its underlying primary dimensions, treating burnout as a multidimensional construct, not a single explanatory term' (p. 293).

In the light of the research they have examined they go on to define burnout as 'a response to chronic emotional stress with components:

- Emotional and/or physical exhaustion;

- Lowered job productivity;

- Over-depersonalisation' (p. 293).

This definition of burnout appears to have much in common with what has been described as 'professional depression' by Oswin (1978) and 'staff institutionalisation' by Raynes, Pratt & Roses (1979). Firth suggests that varying aspects of the burnout syndrome will occur depending on how different personality types attempt to cope with the feelings raised by difficulty, failure or frustration.

The above research would seem to indicate the possibility that those who displace their feelings outwardly as workers, might respond with aggression or the depersonalisation of those they are supposed to be helping, while those who turn their feelings inwards may become depressed.

In summary the relationship between depression, stress and burnout is not at all clear, though there does seem to be some possible links. As regards depression and burnout, it appears that professional depression could be a response by certain workers who are experiencing burnout.

These possible links need to be born in mind when attacking the problem of professional depression.

Treatment Of Depression

In treating depression there are two major approaches used. One approach aims at major, indepth, personality change while the other approach is of a more supportive type. The first approach includes the long term psychotherapies, while the second approach includes short term therapies and behaviour change strategies as well as a number of group activities. These two broad approaches are not mutually exclusive and are sometimes used together in the treatment of depression.

These two categories can be further broken down into five types of interventions. These 5 types of interventions are broad categories showing only one way of giving an overview of the types of help useful in a variety of situations of depression. The aim here is to give an idea of the content of such interventions rather than exactly labeling all the approaches. Such interventions may go under a variety of different, more precise, clinical titles such as psychotherapy, counseling or social skills training.

These five broad approaches are as follows:

- **Grief Therapy**
  This approach encourages the expression of the grief component in the depressed feelings following a major loss or bereavement.

- **Cognitive Therapy**
  This involves a sensitive probing of the person's experiences, enabling them to discover logical errors and false world views that are associated with their depression, and then helping them to build alternative, positive ways of thinking, feeling and acting.

- **Behavioural Therapy**
  Has the aim of extinguishing depressive behaviours and rewarding (reinforcing) non-depressive behaviour.

- **Pastoral Counseling**
  This is used where there is a crisis of meaning, hope, purpose or faith, usually of a spiritual nature. It is often helpful in dealing with questions of guilt and forgiveness.

- **Physical Therapies**
  These approaches include anti-depressants, such as the tricyclics and monoamine oxidase inhibitors, medication such as lithium, as well as electro-convulsive therapy (ECT).

White comments on the reluctance of many people with depressive disorders to use medication or other physical therapies, as follows: '*Most of us would probably prefer either to give or to receive help by psychotherapy than by medication ... It makes us uneasy to think that we are dependent on the electrochemical functioning of our brains and that we are not altogether in control of our destinies. Nevertheless, we must face the constraints of reality*' (p. 193).

White is at pains to make the point that medication serves not to control the minds of depressed people but to restore to them a control that has been impaired.

ECT is a form of physical therapy that has been proven effective when used appropriately. White comments that '*it is clear that the much feared "shock treatment" administered under modern conditions is the safest and most effective treatment for serious depression*' (p. 217).

Some of these five intervention approaches may be used together or also be supplemented, where appropriate, with supportive, group or family and marital therapy.

Professional Depression

As previously mentioned, professional helpers, such as social workers, doctors, priests and ministers, nurses, teachers or the police in their caring role, display many of the characteristics of personality found in those suffering from depression; they are caring, concerned and committed, as noted by Flach. Such personal attributes, on the one hand, are the very basis on which helping is built and on the other hand, these very admirable and necessary qualities may make such persons more open to the effects of depression.

These personal qualities may be further effected by the context in which such helping professionals work; often with difficult people in deprived situations undergoing traumatic life experiences. The possibilities for significant depression to appear in helping professionals in such situations are quite real.

Tragically, when professional helpers, strongly socialised in their roles as carers, become depressed, they often experience more difficulty than the average person in seeking professional help and using this help properly. *'Depressed counsellors find themselves at sea, they need to be resilient and confident to counsel well ... Therefore counsellors should themselves both seek help when they are depressed and trust the judgement of the persons they seek out'* (White, p. 227).

This difficulty in seeking help arises for a number of reasons:

- A still lingering stigma attached to being depressed, seeing it as a sign of weakness and a source of embarrassment, especially if it is in response to a violent incident;

- A belief that depression will not affect a professionally trained carer. Depression is seen as something that happens to others;

- Shame at the thought of being dependent upon other helpers and upon medication;

- Lack of training in the recognition of depression in self or others;

- A lack of understanding of the positive nature of some aspects of the depression experience.

Hopefully, some of these barriers to seeking help will be overcome as more is learnt about depression and its interaction with other key factors in the Human Service Worker's job and life experience.

Dealing With Professional Depression

There are certain overall principles and practices that should be born in mind when dealing with professional depression. Those experiencing professional depression, or those caring for such professionals, should be aware of such strategies.

Firstly, it should be realised that depression happens to almost every helper at some point in their career and it may differ in form and severity from worker to worker. Such realities need to be faced and not denied.

Secondly, there is a need to create an accepting atmosphere in which Human Service Workers suffering from depression 'know how and where to find capable professional help when they need it, and to do so without delay and embarrassment'. (Flach, p. 197)

Thirdly, attempts at intervention to break the spiral of depression must be tailored to match the particular type and phase of the depression. Hart suggests differing strategies for the onset , middle and recovery phases as follows.

At the onset of depression Human Service Workers must be trained to identify potentially triggering events or loss situations, to recognise developing symptoms and reality test their perceptions of events with themselves and others. Depression could be triggered here by a loss of a sense of invulnerability after an assault.

In the middle phase of depression the realities of any major losses must be recognised and accepted, with the full process of grieving being allowed to take place. The worker must be then encouraged to go on with life, painful though it still will be. Skills must also be learnt and encouraged in breaking and changing negative perceptions, interpretations and behaviours, and rebuilding many of the shattered assumptions in their world view.

The recovery phase is marked by increasing periods of 'normality' and a growing ability to think and concentrate, even though the low mood may still be present to some extent. Even at this time of increasing hope for the depressed Human Service Worker there are certain dangers to be avoided.

There is the danger that a temporary reoccurrence of a low mood may be even more devastating to the sufferer after experiencing increasing periods of 'normality'. The person needs to be able to accept these mood swings for what they are, a sign that the depression is lifting. Another concern is that a person on medication may stop taking it as they are feeling better and then plunge back into their depression. A final problem may be that as the person begins to think more clearly they may have to face the loss of some of the secondary gains of remaining in the depression. Some of these gains can include relief of responsibility, avoidance of making painful decisions and the gaining of sympathy from others. Facing such realities head on could lead to further relapses into depression.

In the recovery phase, workers need to be encouraged to increase their physical activity and take on reasonable additional responsibilities. They also need to continue to challenge and change negative 'self talk' such as fear of a relapse, and avoid where possible, depression producing situations.

Fourthly, strategies should be evolved to prevent Human Service Workers who have come out of a period of chronic depression from moving back into it again. Such strategies can include modifying workers' value systems, expectations and patterns of behaviour that may lead to depressive states. Modification may here involve dealing with procrastination, difficulty in setting limits and goals, as well as denial, poor self esteem the and worker's overdependence on the opinions and expectations of others.

Fifthly, it should be realised that not all worker depression can be avoided just by changing workers' values, attitudes or behaviours. Often, the working conditions in which the helping takes place are in themselves potentially violent and depressing and a much greater focus on changing the environment, rather than the worker, is needed.

Finally it needs to be noted that the 'pain' of depression need not be a totally negative experience.

The Positive Side Of Depression

Hart expands on this idea of the positive nature of some aspects of depression by seeking to understand depression in terms of conservation of energy, often as the only healthy, normal reaction to many difficult life situations. He suggests (p. 47) that:

... (1) depression, especially in its milder forms is adaptive; it forces us to make important adjustments to our changing and restricted world, (2) depression seems to facilitate the repair of our psyches following the experience of loss, and (3) depression under many circumstances is self limiting.

Rather than viewing depression as a breakdown, the professional helper suffering an affective disorder should try to see it rather as a potential breakthrough. Professional pride, guilt or ignorance should not be allowed to stop the carer from growing through such a 'dark night of the soul'.

Such an attitude, however, should never downplay the very real emotional and physical pain experienced by those Human Service Workers undergoing a depressive episode, particularly as a response to an incident of violence.

With such insights in mind, the next chapter outlines major preventive and supportive strategies needed in dealing with violence against workers.

Chapter Eight. Healing the Helper.

Agency Responses to Violence Against Human Service Workers

In responding to the issue of violence against Human Service Workers there are a number of important issues to be examined. Perhaps the most crucial of these is, simply, whose responsibility is it to deal with the threat or actual acts of violence?

One response to this question is to suggest that all those involved, or potentially involved, in the situation must accept some responsibility. These include the person involved and their family; the assaulted worker and family; their colleagues; and the agency and its administration. It is thus appropriate that both interventive and preventive strategies take into account these differing, and potentially conflicting, perspectives.

It is also clear that responding to the issue of violence against Human Service Workers must address the three interlocking issues of violence prevention, defusion and post trauma support for staff victims. Thus, response strategies must include aspects of education and training, as well as forward planning and the capacity for a quick response during crisis situations, together with ongoing support for victims.

Preventive Strategies

Naturally, any effective response to the issue of assaults against Human Service Workers requires that due consideration be given to the prevention of assaults as well as intervention after assaults have occurred. A number of preventive strategies are suggested by Brown, Bute & Ford and Bowie & Malcolm (1987) and are outlined below.

Staffing Issues

- Sufficient and appropriate staff should be selected and employed;

- New staff should be given a full and appropriate induction into the work situation and the realistic risks involved;

- Staff should be given initial and ongoing training in the identification, prevention and reduction of violence;

- All staff should feel secure, supported and able to admit fears and negative emotions;

- Staff should be given anticipatory information as to what constitutes normal worker reactions to stressful and abusive situations;

- Staff should feel confident in reporting violent incidents to their management and that such reports will be acted upon;

- The agency or organisation must provide clear practice and emergency guidelines for their staff if faced with actual or potential violence.

Working environment

- All public contact areas, interviewing rooms and other facilities should be designed and furnished so as to provide adequate security as well as a comfortable, calming and welcoming environment;

- Alarm systems should be available and staff instructed as to their appropriate use;

- There should be methods developed to send coded messages indicating danger and needed assistance. Staff should be fully trained in how to respond properly to such calls for help;

- Wherever possible, all potential weapons should be excluded from public contact areas.

Staff Management Issues

Brown et. al. also suggest a number of specific agency responsibilities with regard to staff management, namely:

- To keep staff aware of the dangers of particular high risk procedures, work situations and types of people;

- To ensure that workers are not isolated and that help is always readily available;

- High risk situations are allocated to those most able to cope with them;

- Appropriate back up and support must be available to those working in community-based settings or clients' homes;

- Staff need to be made aware of the different approaches needed in working in a community or client based setting as compared with an agency or institutional setting;

- Good communication must be maintained between administration, staff and service users. Also good contacts must be maintained with police and emergency service personnel;

- All staff rosters and staffing combinations need to be worked out to reduce the risk to staff of confrontation or dangerous situations, without curtailing the service.

Long Term Issues

In the light of the sometimes long term nature of victim recuperation and the specialist services involved, good agency practice of long term planning for preventive and support services should also include:

- The training of their own personnel for the assessing, debriefing, counseling and referral of staff victims;

- Training their staff in the follow up and support of staff victims as peer counsellors;

- The use of outside agencies in the assessing of staff trauma and the provision of assistance and advice to co-workers in providing necessary understanding and support for staff victims. Management should maintain good referral networks with external support agencies, government and voluntary (e.g. victim support schemes, legal and information services, unions and counseling services);

- The establishment of employee assistance committees.

Administrators, managers and supervisors also need to be aware that organisational policies, structure and procedures may generate or alleviate situations leading to violence against workers.

Post Trauma Agency Support

Helping the Staff Victim

As with other victims, 'helper' victims may see themselves as weak, helpless, frightened, and needy, and feel as if they have little control over their lives. They may need to mourn their loss of feelings of security and the related sense of control and invulnerability and to overcome a sense of being different from others.

Coping with victimisation involves the worker coming to terms with the effect of these shattered world view assumptions, and re-establishing a conceptual system that will allow the worker to function effectively once again.

This process involves the re-establishment of a world view which can incorporate the worker's recent experience as a victim, without totally abandoning the previously held basic assumptions. These past assumptions need to be re-fashioned in order that they can also accommodate the worker's new experiences.

As indicated, this involves making sense of the event, restoring a sense of control, purpose and trust as well as being able to plan for the future.

Some Intervention Issues

As stated previously, helper-victims may be unwilling to accept the identity of victim or to seek any help, and may use established defences to block out, minimise or negate the event. However, such defences, or coping strategies, used during the event may be adaptive. Therapeutic endeavours that weaken or break down such defences can be extremely counterproductive.

As Lenehan & Turner (1984(suggest, provided an individual's appraisal and defense strategies are assisting them to produce appropriate adaptive responses to the event and cope positively, a major intervention is probably not warranted.

There are currently few guidelines for distinguishing between helpful and unhelpful coping strategies that might be used by Human Service Workers in responding to assaults against them. However, issues such as an individual's existing world view, available social support structures, and current work and life environment. are obviously of considerable consequence in the development of such strategies.

An assumption here is that staff victims are essentially psychologically healthy individuals facing a crisis, that is, they are normal people having a normal reaction to an abnormal situation. If evidence to the contrary is apparent then quite different, and perhaps more intensive, intervention strategies may be warranted.

Staff victims have the same general difficulties in overcoming fear, anxiety, depression and phobic reactions as do other non-helper victims. Hypervigilance, free floating anxiety, irritability, repetitive intrusive thoughts and nightmares are common, as well as feelings of helplessness and desire for a sense of safety and security. Invariably, anger also appears in one form or another. However, it may be repressed or denied and appear as depression, or else displaced onto others, including patients/clients, staff members or significant others.

As has been noted with non-helper victims, the strong emotions experienced immediately after an assault may be difficult to deal with. As a consequence, victims may distance themselves from others who are trying to offer support, and may repress their feelings and experience various psychosomatic symptoms.

Intervention may also be needed with significant others in the staff victim's life, in order to help them understand the staff person's current state and support needs. Such approaches have been used in Australia with the family and friends of bank hold-up victims.

One way of meeting these needs is through the process called called critical incident debriefing.

Critical Incident Intervention and Support

Support needs to be offered in a sensitive and aware fashion straight after the critical incident, the violent act, so as not to induce secondary trauma. As in dealing with any assault victim, those initiating the intervention and support must be aware of their own emotions and possible projections onto staff victims. Pity, condescension, distancing or blaming by supporters is damaging; rather, unqualified empathy and understanding, in the context of peer and organisational support, is crucial.

Early intervention within 24 hours can provide a solid basis for a more successful, rapid resolution of the crisis situation. Staff victims may firstly need help with immediate problem solving and decision making. This may include: providing immediate first aid and medical help; dealing with emergency staff and police; completing medical and legal reports; providing transport and companionship at home. At the same time, the staff person should have immediate, extensive opportunities to talk about their feelings about the assault with their colleagues and superiors. Debriefing in a non-blaming fashion should be available, and provided in a manner that develops the worker's skills for handling future incidents.

Mitchell (1983, 1988) has developed a comprehensive model for doing the above, which he calls Critical Incident Stress Debriefing (CISD), to minimise the negative impact of crisis situations on helpers. The CISD concept is a developing one, with potential application to helper-victims.

A CISD is a psychological and educational group process designed especially for workers, with two purposes in mind. Firstly, the CISD is designed to mitigate the impact of critical incidents on the person. Secondly, the CISD is designed to accelerate recovery in normal people who are experiencing the normal signs, symptoms and reactions to totally abnormal events.

A supportive approach, rather than a therapeutic one, can set a tone for the initial intervention as one of developing mastery and strength without down-playing the extreme trauma experienced. There is a danger that in conveying an expectation of a deep, reactive, emotional trauma, one may create a self-fulfilling prophecy. However, staff should be given information about their own possible responses and feelings as victims, and the acceptability and naturalness of such reactions.

Rather than seeking individual counseling, the staff victim may need or want to discuss the incident and their reaction to it within the work situation and with fellow professionals, and may choose not to see the assault as a personal attack. Thus, if the worker wishes to deal with the assault within the work context and appears to be coping adequately, then clearly, simple support is sufficient intervention.

Such personal support strategies also need to be seen in the context of broader responses which the employer's agency needs to be able to implement.

Agency Responsibilities

To minimise the negative consequences of assaults and violence when they do occur, and to provide optimal assistance to staff victims, some specific guidelines for agency action can be suggested:

- Staff should have immediate, extensive opportunities to talk about their feelings surrounding the assault with colleagues and administrators. Mitchell refers to this process as a defusing;

- Debriefing in a non-blaming fashion should be available within 24 hours and provided in a manner that develops the worker's skills for handling future incidents;

- Staff should be given information about their own possible responses and feelings as victims and the acceptability and naturalness of such reactions;

- Practical help and support should be made available, including offers of ongoing personal protection, a carefully supervised or changed workload or the possibility of job sharing;

- Allowing time off from the job, or time out in an alternative work location, could be another practical response. Help regarding training and seeking other career opportunities may also be needed;

- The staff victim's associates, administrators, co-workers, friends and family, should be made aware of the victim's possible feelings, responses and needs and be helped, wherever necessary, in their support for the assaulted person. These associates and the agency need to remain aware of the long term nature of the recovery from violence and its trauma. Sometimes, more than short term crisis intervention is needed, and intervention might involve the rebuilding of the victim's assumptive world. For example, the possible effects of the assault on changing the staff victim's view of the patient/client and the agency may also need to be recognised and dealt with;

- In order that staff are not further stigmatised for seeking trauma counseling or taking part in violence prevention programs, these programs should be part of a comprehensive continuing education aspect of an organisation's training.

This broader approach could include topics such as induction to the organisation, preventative stress management programs, communication and assertion skills, group and leadership styles, and healthy lifestyle information.

Post Trauma Support by Co-Workers

In the light of the possible danger of secondary trauma being inflicted upon staff victims by colleagues through blaming, distancing, hesitancy or overly emotional reactions, a high level of co-worker awareness and sensitivity needs to be encouraged and maintained.

Mitchell, in his article 'Teaming Up Against Critical Incident Stress', suggests that these problems can be overcome in part by training workers as 'peer counsellors'. He describes peer counsellors as staff members who are trained to provide the first basic support to their traumatised fellow workers. Often they are the ones who let management know that a structured debriefing may be required.

Environmental barriers such as agency or staff indifference to the problem may also make trauma support by co-workers difficult.

Staff Victim Assistance Programs

Potential Barriers to Programs.

Engels & Marsh (1986) point out that many forces work against the acceptance of an employee assistance program by both management and workers.

Many professional helping staff have difficulty seeing themselves as, or accepting the role of, a victim. In addition, since violence is perpetrated by those in their care, staff often do not accept assault as a work related accident, but rather view it as part of the conditions of the job. Thus, this view may excuse the behaviour of the aggressive person and it is often further condoned by the agency through its silence or inaction.

The milieu of the tight knit helping community also may make it difficult for workers to express feelings of fear or uncertainty about those they help and the work situation. This, in turn, makes it hard for individuals or work teams to accept, or actively support, victim assistance schemes for themselves.

Unless an injury makes it difficult for a staff member to stay at work, they often continue on the job trying to minimise the abuse faced until stress and low morale take their toll. Thus, assaulted workers are often left isolated from their peers, feeling apathetic and angry and trying to withdraw.

Another negative force against accepting such schemes is the previously mentioned blaming and distancing attitude displayed by co-workers. For workers to admit to the necessity for such assistance programs for others, let alone themselves, once again challenges the worker's feelings of invulnerability.

In the light of potential resistance by staff to such programs they should be presented as part of an overall staff education and preventative health program as previously mentioned.

By including aggression management skills amongst such topics, workers are given preventative information and are not stigmatised for attending such courses. Also, in this way, the question of violence in the workplace is not sensationalised and the unnecessary arousing of staff anxiety is avoided.

However, despite such barriers, successful employee assistance programs for victims of violence have been implemented and can serve as useful models. Some programs for armed hold up and bank robbery victims also have much to teach those initiating such services in the health, welfare and community service sectors.

Roy Bailey (1985) outlines a professional support system for nurses and other medical personnel, to combat stress. This could serve as a model, with some modifications, for the above suggested aggression trauma management programs as part of a continuing education format. Such a support system could undertake many of the functions outlined previously.

Obviously, such comprehensive programs may be more easily sponsored by large medical and welfare organisations. Smaller services may need greater access to outside counseling and support services in a flexible way in order to meet the needs of their own staff.

Implementing Assistance Programs

In the light of the above, and having regard for the particular needs and responses of staff victims, an employee assistance program should include a number of different services. These may include medical attention; trauma support and counseling; legal advice; and information on compensation, workers' rights and other health and safety issues.

Engels and Marsh suggest the formation of a permanent committee in each agency to oversee such programs and to guarantee the rights of both service users and employees. This helps to make such programs the joint responsibility and appropriate function of both management and staff within an organisation.

They suggest that the role and tasks of such committees should comprise:

•   The creation and monitoring of an on-call team to deal with violent incidents;

•   Making sure that guidelines and procedures for dealing with violent people and employee victims are formulated and carried out;

•   The collection of incident reports and the collation of appropriate strategies;

- The careful examination of each violent episode, with appropriate recommendations about future action and an evaluation of their outcomes.

These committee responsibilities as outlined by Engels and Marsh are only some of the wide ranging aspects involved in the implementation of such employee assistance programs.

Aggressor Assistance Programs

Though the focus in this book has been on helping the Human Service Worker in their attempts to prevent and defuse violent situations, the aim of any intervention must equally be the welfare of both the other person and the worker. So there also obviously needs to be ways made available to help potential and actual aggressors control and deal with their own violent impulses. Details about such programs are beyond the scope of this book but opportunities should be accessible to actual or potential aggressors, whenever possible, especially where workers may have an ongoing work relationship with such people.

However, while attempting to do this we should bear in mind Aronson's (1984) comment that frustration, caused by deprivation, is the major instigator of aggressive behaviour and in the light of this, ways need to be found to reduce the injustices that produce the frustrations that erupt into violent acts.

If the worker is able to understand the other person's aggressive behaviour as often being the result of frustration caused by unjust conditions, then they may be able to help them channel such responses into more effective strategies rather than condemning them. Thus, the helper is not only respecting the other's human rights, but is also teaching them to demand these rights for themselves through a more effective protest against social injustice and inequality.

However, even with above the positive interpretation and responses, it is unlikely that violent assaults against human service workers can be eliminated entirely, especially in a context of apparently increasing levels of violent behaviour in the general community.

It is imperative, therefore, that helping professionals attempt to overcome their illusions of invulnerability, and make themselves aware of this issue, and its relevance for both themselves and their colleagues. Thus, they can assist their various employers to develop and implement strategies that will hopefully minimise both the incidence of the problem and its damaging consequences to individual helpers. However, the onus for taking appropriate action should not lie just with the individual workers. An equally heavy responsibility to take the major initiatives lies with the human service organisations and their management structures. Without such initiatives, responses by individuals are likely to be partial and fragmented, and thus ineffectual.

Now in chapter nine is concluded *A Soft Answer*! Here, an alternative way to resolve violence is used, one that recognises the above mentioned frustrations, caused by loss, that may lead to aggression.

Chapter Nine. A Soft Answer (part two).

A split second before he moved, someone shouted 'Hey!' It was ear-splitting. I remember being struck by the strangely joyous, lilting quality of it, as though you and a friend had been searching diligently for something and had suddenly stumbled upon it. 'Hey!'

I wheeled to my left, the drunk spun to his right. We both stared down at a little old Japanese. He must have been well into his seventies. He took no notice of me but beamed delightedly at the labourer, as though he had a most important, most welcome secret to share.

'C'mere,' the old man said in an easy vernacular, beckoning to the drunk. 'C'mere and talk with me.' He waved his hand lightly. The big man followed, as if on a string. He planted his feet belligerently in front of the old man, towering threateningly over him. 'Talk to you,' he roared above the clanking wheels. 'Why the hell should I talk to you?'

The old man continued to beam at the labourer. There was not a trace of fear or resentment about him. 'What'cha been drinking?' he asked lightly, his eyes sparkling with interest.

'I been drinking sake,' the labourer bellowed back, 'and it's none of your goddam business!' Flecks of spittle spattered the old man.

'Oh, that's wonderful,' the old man said with delight. 'Absolutely wonderful! You see, I love sake, too. Every night, me and my wife (she's seventy-six, you know), we warm up a little bottle of sake and take it out into the garden, and we sit on the old wooden bench that my grandfather's first student made for him. We watch the sun go down, and we look to see how our persimmon tree is doing, and we worry whether it will recover from those ice storms we had last winter. Persimmons do not do well after ice storms, although I must say that ours has done rather better than I expected, especially when you consider the poor quality of the soil. Still, it is most gratifying to watch when we take our sake and go out to enjoy the evening—even when it rains!' He looked up at the labourer, eyes twinkling, happy to share his delightful information.

As he struggled to follow the intricacies of the old man's conversation, the drunk's face began to soften. His fists slowly unclenched. 'Yeah,' he said slowly, 'I love persimmons, too...' His voice trailed off.

'Yes,' said the old man, smiling, 'and I'm sure you have a wonderful wife.'

'No,' replied the labourer. 'My wife died.' He hung his head. Very gently, swaying with the motion of the train, the big man began to sob. 'I don't got no wife. I don't got no home. I don't got no job. I don't got no money. I don't got nowhere to go.' Tears rippled down his cheeks, and a spasm of pure despair rippled through his body. Above the baggage rack a four-colour ad trumpeted the virtues of suburban luxury living.

Now it was my turn. Standing there in my well-scrubbed youthful innocence, my make-this-world-safe-for-democracy righteousness, I suddenly felt dirtier than the drunk was.

Just then the train arrived at my stop. The platform was packed, and the crowd surged into the car as soon as the doors opened. Maneuvering my way out, I heard the old man cluck sympathetically. 'My, my,' he said with undiminished delight. 'That is a very difficult predicament, indeed. Sit down here and tell me about it.'

I turned my head for one last look. The labourer was sprawled like a sack on the seat, his head in the old man's lap. The old man looked down on him all compassion and delight, one hand softly stroking the filthy, matted head.

As the train pulled away, I sat down on a bench. What I had wanted to do with muscle and meanness had been accomplished with a few kind words. I had seen Aikido tried in combat, and the essence of it was love, as the founder had said. I would have to practise the art with an entirely different spirit.

It would be a long time before I could speak about the resolution of conflict.

'A soft and gentle answer turns away wrath
but a harsh word stirs up anger.'

Proverbs 15:1

A Personal Conclusion

... I still have a dream, because you know, you can't give up in life. If you lose hope, somehow you lose that vitality that keeps life moving, you lose courage to be, that quality that helps you go on in spite of it all.

I have a dream that one day men will rise up and come to see that they are made to live together as brothers...I still have a dream today that one day war will come to an end, that men will beat their swords into ploughshares and their spears into pruning hooks, and neither will they study war anymore ... With this faith we will be able to speed up the day when there will be peace on earth and goodwill toward men.

Martin Luther King, 1968

Like Martin Luther King, I also have dreams of peace on earth, goodwill toward men. But I also know that such peace does not just happen, but involves people of goodwill who seek peace and pursue it.

We all, as members of a society, have a responsibility to find ways of lessening violence, in all its forms. Violence includes racism, sexism, ageism, poverty, oppression and environmental pollution. Let us strive to be free of these aspects in ourselves as we also, in a practical way, attempt to release others from the oppression and frustrations that are often expressed through violence.

Vaughan Bowie
Christmas 1988

About This Book

This book is part of an integrated violence management training package that has been developed by the author. This package includes a teaching video, *Coping With Violence* plus a facilitator's manual and participants' workbooks.

The video contains basic information about violence prevention strategies as well as three short scenes of escalating violence in health and welfare settings. These vignettes can be used for analysis and discussion of appropriate intervention strategies.

Information about the *Coping With Violence* training package as well as provision of inservice training on these, and related, issues, can be obtained from the author:

Vaughan Bowie
The School of Community and Welfare Studies,
University of Western Sydney, Macarthur,
P.O. Box 555 Campbelltown, N.S.W. 2560
Australia

Tel : (02) 772 9200   FAX : (02) 774 3649

The author is also interested in corresponding with anyone who has used or developed training packages related to the issue of coping with aggression and violence against Human Service Workers.

BIBLIOGRAPHY

American Psychiatric Association (1980),*The Diagnostic and Statistical Manual of Mental Disorders*,(3rd ed.) (DSM III), Washington DC, American Psychiatric Association.

Aronson, E. (1984), *The Social Animal*, Freeman, New York.

Bailey, R. (1985) *Coping with Stress in Caring*, Blackwell Scientific Publications.,UK.

Bernstein, H.A. (1981), 'Survey of Threats and Assaults Directed towards Psychotherapists', *American Journal of Psychotherapy*, 35, pp. 542–549.

Bard, M. and Sangrey, D. (1979), *The Crime Victims Book*, Basic Books, N.Y.

Bowie, V. (1982), 'Burnout in the Helping Professions' in *Advances in Behavioural Medicine*, (ed. Sheppard, J.), Cumberland College of Health Sciences, Volume 2, pp. 189–198, Sydney.

Bowie, V. (1987), 'Stress and Aggression Levels in a Social Welfare Agency', (Unpublished paper), School of Community and Welfare Studies, Macarthur Institute of Higher Education, Sydney.

Bowie, V. (1988a), 'Depression and Human Service Workers', (Unpublished paper), School of Community and Welfare Studies, Macarthur Institute of Higher Institute, Sydney.

Bowie, V. (1988b), 'Coping with Violence Against Human Service Workers', Paper presented at Conference Dealing with Stress and Trauma in Emergency Services, Social Biology Resource Centre, Melbourne.

Bowie, V. and Malcolm, J. (1989), 'Violence Against Human Service Workers', in *Advances in Behavioural Medicine*, (ed. Sheppard, J.) Cumberland College of Health Sciences, Volume 6, Chapter 11, pp. 157–186, Sydney.

Brown, R., Bute, S., and Ford, P. (1986), *Social Workers at Risk*, Macmillan.

Dobson, T. and Shepherd-Chow (1981), *Safe and Alive*, J.P. Tarcher Inc. Los Angeles.

Dubin, W., Wilson, S. and Mercer, C. (1988), 'Assault Against Psychiatrists in Outpatient Settings', *Journal of Clinical Psychiatry*, 49:9, September, pp. 338–345.

Dubrow, R. (1988), 'Suicide Among Social Workers in Rhode Island,' *Journal of Occupational Medicine*, Vol. 30, 3, March, pp. 211–213.

Engels, F. and Marsh, S. (1986), 'Helping the Employee Victim of Violence in Hospitals', *Hospital and Community Psychiatry*, 37 (2), pp. 159–162.

Everstein, D. and Everstein, L. (1983), *People in Crisis*, Bruner/Mazel, New York.

Field, G. (1988), *Violent Trends in the Eighties*, Central District Ambulance Sydney, Australia.

Firth, H., McIntee, J., McKeown P. and Britton P., 'Burnout and Professional Depression: Related Concepts?', *Journal of Advanced Nursing*, 11, (1986), pp. 633–641.

Flach, F., (1986), *The Secret Strength of Depression*, Bantam Books, NY.

Frederick, C. (1980), 'Effects of Natural vs. Human Induced Violence', in Kivens, L. (ed.) *Services for Survivors, Evaluation and Change*, pp. 71–75, Minneapolis Medical Research Foundation, Minneapolis MN.

Freudenberger, H., and Richardson, G., (1985) *Burn Out*, Arrow Books London.

Gaskin, J. (1986), 'In Trouble', *The Canadian Nurse*, April pp. 31–34.

Hart, A. (1984), *Coping with Depression in the Ministry and Other Helping Professions*, Word Books, Texas.

Hayes, S. and Fisher, C. (1987), 'Burnout Amongst Gynaecologists and General Practitioners', Draft Paper, Department of Behavioural Sciences, Sydney University, Australia.

Hildreth, A., Derogatis, L. and McCusker, K. (1971), 'Body Buffer Zone and Violence: A Reassessment and Confirmation', *American Journal of Psychiatry*, 127, pp. 1641–1645.

Horwell, F. (1985), 'The Causes and Control of Violence', *Court Counsellors Bulletin*, Aug, Vol 2, 3, pp. 15–27.

Holden, R.J. (1985), 'Aggression Against Nurses', *The Australian Nurses Journal*, 15 (3), Sep, pp. 44–48.

Industrial Relations Service (1979), 'Violence at Work', *Health and Safety Bulletin*, 39, March.

Infanto, J. and Musingo, S. (1985), 'Assaultive injuries amongst staff with and without training in aggression control techniques' in *Hospital and Community Psychiatry*, 36, pp. 1312–1314.

Janoff-Bulman R. (1985), 'The Aftermath of Victimization: Rebuilding Shattered Assumptions' in Figley (ed.) *Trauma and Its Wake*, pp. 15–35 Brunner/Mazel, NY.

Kahn, A.S. (1984), *Victims of Crime and Violence: Final Report of the APA Task Force on the Victims of Crime and Violence*, American Psychological Association, Washington, DC.

Kalogerakis, M.G. (1971), 'The Assaultive Psychiatric Patient', *Psychiatric Quarterly*, 45, pp. 372–381.

Kaplan, H.I. and Saddock, B.J. (1981), *Modern Synopsis of Comprehensive Textbook of Psychiatry III*, (3rd ed.), Williams & Wilkins, London .

King H. (1987), 'The Influence of Perceived Organizational Power, Responsibility and Autonomy on Alcoholism Amongst Social Workers', *Social Work Research and Abstracts* , Vol 23, Fall, pp. 33

King, M. L. Jr. (1968), *The Trumpet of Conscience*, Harper & Row Publishers, New York.

Krupnick, J. L., and Horowitz, M. J. (1981), 'Victims of Violence: Psychological Responses, Treatment Implications', *Evaluation & Change*, special issue, pp. 42–46

Lenehan, G. P., and Turner, J. (1984), 'Treatment of Staff Victims of Violence' in Turner J. (ed), *Violence in a Medical Care Setting: A Survival Guide*, pp. 251–260, Aspen Publications Maryland,.

Lerner, M. (1980), *The Belief in a Just World*, Plenum Press.

Levy B. and Brown V. (1984), 'Strategies for crisis intervention with victims of violence' in *Violent Individuals & Families*, Saunders S., et al (eds.), Charles C. Thomas.

Lifton, R. J. (1983), *The Broken Connection*, Basic Books.

Link, B. (1988), *The Working Conditions of Sheriffs Officers*, Occupational Health and Safety Committee Report, Office of the Sheriff, Sydney, NSW.

McCue, J. (1982), 'The Effect of Stress on Physicians and Their Medical Practice', *New England Journal of Medicine*, Feb, 25, pp. 458–463.

Madden, D. J., Lion, J. R., and Penna, M. W. (1976), 'Assaults on Psychiatrists by Patients', *American Journal of Psychiatry*, 133, pp. 422–425.

Mason, L. J. (1980), *Guide to Stress Reduction*, Peace Press, California.

Mitchell, J.T. (August 1986,) 'Teaming Up Against Critical Incident Stress', *Chief Fire Executive*, pp. 24,26,84.

Mitchell, J.T. and Resnik, H. L. P. (1981), *Emergency Response to Crisis*, Prentice Hall.

Mitchell, J.T. (1989), *Emergency Services Stress*, Prentice Hall: A Brady Book, Engelwood Cliffs, NY.

Mitchell, J.T. , 'When disaster strikes ... The critical incident debriefing process', J.E.M.S. Jan, 1983, pp. 36–39.

Mitchell, J.T. (1988), 'The how to's and what not's of putting together a CISD team', Paper presented at the conference Dealing with Stress and Trauma in Emergency Services, Social Biology Resource Centre, Melbourne.

Mitchell, P. (1988), 'Reclassifying depressive illness, will the new DSM–III and DSM–lll–R classifications help?' *Current Therapeutics*, October, pp. 13–22.

Monahan, J. (1984), The prediction of violent behaviour: toward a second generation of theory & policy', *American Journal of Psychiatry* 141, 1, Jan, pp 10–15.

Moran, J. (1984), 'Teaching the management of violent behavior to nursing staff: a health care model' in Turner, J. (ed.), *Violence in the Medical Care Setting: A Survival Guide*, Aspen, Rockville, MD.

National Association of Local Government Officers (1981), *Safety Representative Bulletin*, 4, London.

National Organization for Victim Assistance – N.O.V.A. (Undated), *Crisis and Stress*, Washington, DC.

Oswin, M. (1978), *Children Living in Long Stay Hospitals.*, Heinemann, London.

Perlman, B. and Hartman, E. (1982), 'Burnout: Summary and Future Research', *Human Relations*, Vol 55 (4), pp. 283–305.

Peterson, C. and Seligman, M. (1983), 'Learned Helplessness and Victimization', *Journal of Social Issues*, 39 (2), pp. 103–116.

Raphael, Beverley (1987), *When Disaster Strikes*, Basic Books, NY.

Raphael, B, Singh, B. and Bradbury L. (1980), 'Disaster: The Helpers' Perspective', *Medical Journal of Australia*, 2: 445–447.

Raynes N., Pratt, M. and Roses, S. (1979), *Organizational Structure and Care of the Mentally Retarded*, Croom Helm, London.

Rowett, C. (1986), *Violence in Social Work*, University of Cambridge Institute of Criminology.

Schultz, L. G. (1987), 'The Social Worker as a Victim of Violence', *Social Casework News & Views*, April, 240–244.

Shick-Tryon, G. (1986), 'Abuse of therapists by patients: a national survey', *Professional Psychology: Research & Practice*, 17 (4), 357–363.

Siann, G. (1985), *Accounting for Aggression, Perspectives on Aggression and Violence*, Allen and Unwin, London.

Smith, P. (1983), *Professional Assault Training*, (Unpublished) Citrus Heights, California.

Swedish Union of Social Workers, Personnel and Public Administration (1987), *Violence and Intimidation in Social Work*, (Unpublished paper), Stockholm, Sweden.

Symonds, M. (1976), 'The Rape Victim: Psychological Patterns of Response', *American Journal of Psychoanalysis*, 36, pp. 19–26.

Thackery, M. (1987a), 'Clinician confidence in coping with patient aggression: assessment and enhancement', *Pro-

fessional Psychology: Research and Practice, Vol 18, No 1, pp. 57–60.

Thackery, M. (1987b), *Therapeutics for Aggression: Psychological/Physical Crisis Intervention*, Human Sciences Press, New York.

Thompson, G. (1983), *Verbal Judo*, Charles C. Thomas, Illinois.

Weiner, R. and Crosby, J. (1986), *Handling Violence and Aggression*, Adolescents Project Training Papers, N.C.V.C.C.O., London.

Whitman, R. M., Armao, B. B., and Dent, O. B. (1976), 'Assault on the therapist', *American Journal of Psychiatry*, 133, 426–429.

White, J. (1982), *The Masks Of Melancholy*, Inter-Varsity Press, England.

Wilson, J., Smith, W. and Johnson, S. (1985), 'A comparative analysis of post traumatic stress syndrome among individuals exposed to different stressor events' in Figley, C. R., *Trauma and its Wake: The Study and Treatment of Post-Traumatic Stress Disorder*, Brunner Mazel, pp. 142–172.

INDEX